DARE
TO BE
FAIR

**HOW TO KNOW YOUR WORTH AND
BUILD YOURSELF A BETTER FINANCIAL FUTURE**

AMANDA REDMAN

Copyright

Disclaimer

The views expressed in this book are the personal views of the author and do not constitute financial advice. No investment, tax, legal or insurance advice is intended or given, and any ideas should never be used without first assessing your financial situation, and consulting a qualified adviser if needed. Investments are subject to risk factors that may not be discussed completely, or at all, in this book. The value of an investment may fall as well as rise and you may get back less than you invested. The levels and bases of taxation and reliefs from taxation can change at any time. Tax relief is dependent on individual circumstances. Taxation and legislation referred to are relevant for the UK only, in the 2021-22 tax year.

Copyright Acknowledgements

The author wishes to thank the following for permission to reproduce copyright material.

Jane Portas, Creator of 6 Moments That Matter, Co-Founder Insuring Women's Futures (a programme hosted by the Chartered Insurance Institute) and author of The Women's Risks in Life Report Series, initially published by the Chartered Insurance Institute. For details of 6 Moments That Matter and the full series of works, see:

www.6momentsthatmatter.com

Every effort has been made to trace rights holders, but if any have been inadvertently overlooked, the publishers would be pleased to make the necessary arrangements at the first opportunity.

To every woman, with strong roots and wings,
who wants to live her best possible life

Contents

Table of Figures

Acknowledgements

I want to thank all the women who were happy to be interviewed for this book. Your insights and experiences have helped shape my ideas.

Special thanks to my beta-readers who took time out of their busy lives to read my first manuscript, and provided invaluable feedback to make the book much better than it would otherwise have been: Tania Howarth, Siobhan Stirling, Dawn Gibson, Joanna Morrow, Louise Cruttenden, Ella Rees, Sharron Boyce, Jessica Fearnley, Iola Palmer-Stirling, Caroline Watson, Denise Searle and Sandhya Iyer.

It's been a great experience working with Mitali Deypurkaystha, book-writing coach and mentor, whose programme galvanised me into creating a coherent book from all the thoughts and ideas in my head. Thank you to Coral McCloud for the cover design, and Hania Nevill for editing the book.

A big thank you to Sharp Minds Communications and Girl Friday Graphics for your marketing and graphic design input. You are a valuable source of continual support in my local business network.

Thank you to all the great male and female colleagues and bosses I've had the pleasure of working with along the way, showing me the best way forward (and also to the bad ones who have shown me how not to do things).

A final thank you to my financial planning team, you are all brilliant, and to my family, for putting up with my Covid lockdown project, and the many hours spent working on it; especially to my husband Mike, whose support and self-assured outlook on life has nurtured my own roots and wings, and enabled me to write this book.

Introduction

"I am my own woman."

– **Evita Peron**

About Me

The Missing Ring

I was 22, waiting to be interviewed for a graduate marketing role at a blue-chip brand company. I was in my final year at university and had worked hard to get there.

I had attended my local primary school on a council estate, where I was the first person in the school to ever pass the eleven plus exam. I had gone on to Chelmsford Grammar School for Girls, which was an hour away from home on the bus. I had always enjoyed learning, was conscientious and worked hard. After A levels, I had studied languages at Selwyn College, Cambridge.

I really wanted this graduate job. I had recently got engaged to my first husband and was excited about what the future had in store. But, as I was sitting waiting to be interviewed, I had a sudden instinct to take off my engagement ring. I removed it and put it in my pocket.

I didn't want to reveal that I was getting married, in case it was misinterpreted by my future employer. I didn't want to risk them rejecting me, because they thought I might go off and have babies. It was an uncomfortable moment, but I trusted my instinct.

It was the early 1990s then, and 30 years on, as a 52-year-old, happily married to my second husband Mike, with our 12-year-old daughter and 23-year-old son from my first marriage, I'm wondering whether much has changed.

As my son has been interviewing this year for graduate roles, with corporate employers, I'm wondering whether any of his female friends have the same concern that I did.

And in 10 years, will my daughter face the same indecision? Can a young woman be ambitious, have a successful career, *and* be a good mum, in the eyes of a corporate employer and of society?

Being Good Enough

This question is at the heart of one of my life's defining moments. In 1990, when my fiancé and I announced our engagement to my parents, they did not welcome the news. They expressed doubts, as to whether I could have a successful career and be a good mum at the same time. They were concerned I was getting married too young, but I interpreted it as them challenging my capabilities and my freedom to make my own decisions. As someone who has always felt determined and independent, this was a strong challenge indeed.

It caused a huge row and rift at the time, but with the benefit of hindsight and some maturity, I now understand that their doubts were not really about me as an individual. They were the result of their upbringing and the learned beliefs picked up from their parents, rather than misgivings about whether *I* was good enough to do both.

However, from then on, I took it as a personal challenge to prove to my parents, myself and the world that I *could* be successful, in both my career and with my family.

I was blind to this as my driving force at the time, I was just determined to carry on doing my best, making my own decisions and being independent.

I soon became the main breadwinner and that has continued throughout my life. That, combined with my determined streak, has resulted in me always feeling self-sufficient financially, by being able to rely on myself and my resources.

I appreciate this is not every woman's experience, so I want to share my learnings from this, to benefit others.

My Guilty Secret

Now I'm going to share something with you that's hard to write down in black and white, because of the judgement society makes, but this is the truth:

Work has always come before being a mum for me. Enjoying my work and feeling fulfilled makes me a better mum I believe, despite the challenges it presents.

I have never wanted to sacrifice my career because I'm a mum. However, I have adapted it to achieve the right balance, sometimes because I had to in the corporate environment, and sometimes because I wanted to (when I chose to run my own business).

Other women, other friends have made different choices to achieve the right balance for them, and of course, there is no right or wrong here, but the consequences of our choices as working mums are something we need to fully understand.

I want to open your eyes to the long-term financial consequences of the decisions we make once we start a family.

The Token Tart

I had a very successful corporate career with the blue-chip company I joined – and I did wear my engagement ring once I started working there. I worked my way up the ladder from marketing trainee to European Marketing Director. Most of the time it was hugely enjoyable and I got to travel to far more countries than I would otherwise have done. Regular work trips to cities such as Paris, Madrid, Turin and Warsaw were real highlights, getting to appreciate the culture of the people I was working with, and seeing how different some of the attitudes towards working mums can be in neighbouring countries.

There was a lot to love about my first career, but there were certain things that were issues for me at the time, and which I have since realised were not fair or equitable.

For example, I was treated differently to a male colleague when we were promoted at the same time - he was promoted by two grades, and I was promoted by one. I believe his promotion was based on his future potential, whilst my promotion was based on my track record.

This hit me hard at the time and I remember being very upset, even though being promoted at all was a significant achievement. Nevertheless, it just didn't feel quite fair, and the reasons I was given for the different approaches didn't ring true.

Another example is in the different experiences I had returning from my two periods of maternity leave. When I returned to work the first time, I was promoted into my new role, which was fantastic. The second time around it was a different story. I foolishly agreed to take a role below my grade, until a more senior role became available, and it just didn't happen.

Over the following years, I felt the company was no longer able to support my ambitions and give me the opportunities I needed to progress my career; so when I had the option to take redundancy, I took it.

I left because a lot of things, by that stage, had started to grind me down. The corporate politics were significant as the company expanded and operated globally. There was an underlying and continual challenge of being treated, subtly, differently as a female senior leader. In some roles and leadership teams, I felt like the "token tart," a female who had been appointed to tick the diversity box.

One such experience was taking a sideways step out of Marketing and into Sales. I was the first and only female director of a Customer Business Unit, responsible for working with retailers in the UK and Germany. I was left to sink or swim, with little support and no training. My boss used to walk past my office door without saying hello, on his way to talk to his buddy next door, about their golf game at the weekend.

Ultimately though, it was the impact of taking a career break twice, and the effect this had on my pay and career progression, that were deciding factors in me leaving corporate employment.

The gender pay gap continues to exist, even when comparing like-for-like roles. It may be shrinking but it's still there – with alarming persistency and consistency across so many roles.

What my second career has now taught me are the truly devastating consequences of this pay gap for many women in later life. How it snowballs into a gender pensions gap, meaning that generations of women are retiring in poverty.

The Killer Question

I now run my own Financial Planning business which I set up eight years ago after retraining. I have fulfilled my desire to be my own boss, and do things my way, and a few years ago, took on the very real responsibility of employing other people.

I've never been happier. The difference we make to our clients' financial futures makes me very proud. Working with over 200 clients, managing their savings, pensions and investments to help them live their best possible life, is a privilege; one that my team and I all enjoy hugely and take very seriously.

Running my own business has meant that I can benefit from a true meritocracy, where what I earn is driven by my hard work and expertise, not by corporate HR practices such as length of service, time in-role, or who my senior sponsor is.

More and more women are successfully starting up businesses, for similar reasons. However leaving the corporate workplace in significant numbers is not going to create the changes needed within these organisations, to achieve a truly diverse, well supported and fairly paid workforce.

I now advise women across a broad range of financial planning areas and have become an expert in pensions and retirement planning.

Even though the mere mention of the word 'pension' can make people's eyes glaze over, it is usually the main way of funding your life after you stop working. It's therefore, one of *the* most important things in the world, especially as, apparently, we're all going to live to 100.

It couldn't be more important.

So why do too many women ignore it and stick their head in the sand, or leave it to their partners to think about and manage?

What my second career has now shown me are the true financial consequences of the decisions we make during our working life — particularly working part-time or taking a career break — and how oblivious we are to the long-term implications.

Today, on average, women retire with just 20% of the pension wealth of men at age 65[1].

And the real killer question is: why don't women know this?

My Reason for Writing

The aim of Dare To Be Fair is to make women aware of the financial disadvantages that can occur in later life if they do not take proactive steps to avoid them.

Anyone not following a traditional male linear career path — and therefore especially women — can suffer from the effects of the very real, albeit unintended, pay gap.

However, the gender pay gap leads to something even more pernicious: an even wider *pensions* gap for women looking to retire in their mid-60s.

A report authored by Jane Portas, co-founder of Insuring Women's Futures, a market-wide programme to improve women's financial resilience, hosted by the Chartered Insurance Institute, illustrated how the gap in men and women's pensions accumulates throughout life. As quoted above, it reported that on average, a woman retires with only 20% of the pension wealth of a man at age 65.

This means for every £10,000 in a man's pension pot, the woman has just £2,000.

How can it be fair that this gap is so wide? That when a woman decides to have a family and raise her children — often during the formative years of her career, because that's what Mother Nature has determined — she is rewarded in later life by having just one-fifth of the money to live on compared to what men have.

This is not the only reason that leads to this outcome, but it is a significant one.

I want to raise awareness of this pension gap, to encourage and inspire women of all ages to get involved in planning their financial future. And to exert pressure for change in the workplace, supported by legislation where needed.

Fairness is a core value of mine and a strong driver of my thinking and behaviour. I'm frustrated that not enough has changed in the 30 years since I first entered the corporate workplace.

I want the next generation of career women, my son's female friends, to experience greater fairness in the workplace than I did — in the way their skills and future potential are assessed, in the way they are promoted and in the way they are paid.

Financial fairness is so important because money gives you choices. Money is the means to an end, and for us all to have the best life possible, we need to have enough money to give us that freedom of choice.

> *Financial fairness is so important because money gives you choices*

Personal Yet Not Unique

The content of the book is based on my personal experiences and is therefore anecdotal.

Whilst I do quote some facts and figures throughout the book, this is to provide context rather than provide an academic study.

This means that my examples, experiences and opinions are based on my own life.

The scenarios I describe are not intended to minimise other women's experiences or relationships. For example, as a heterosexual, married woman, I best relate to and therefore describe long-term relationships between men and women. However, I hope (and believe) there is relevance here for every relationship, and for those of you reading this book who are single.

To try and facilitate this, I refer to the other half as "partner" throughout the book, not intending to be specific on marital status, and I use "he" as a proxy for the partner's gender.

The other main example is that I take learnings from working in a corporate office environment. I have never worked in the public sector, so do not feel I can comment on workplace practices there.

I know that many of my personal experiences are mine alone, but I also know that many aspects will resonate with your own life. Although my circumstances are individual, they are not unique.

I believe there is a universality to what I have observed. I am validated in this by hearing what my clients tell me, as I now advise and work with women across all ages and personal situations.

What You'll Get From Reading This Book

The book covers a broad range of topics, such as:

- women's money mindset and personal finances
- workplace culture and practices that influence how much we earn and how far we get in our career

- social and legislative issues and opportunities, to improve fairness for women financially

As well as hopefully being thought-provoking, it's intended to be a manual for you to use to assess your situation and to open your eyes to the reality of how things are.

It will help you prepare for conversations with your partner, your family, friends, your employer or employees and maybe your MP.

I hope it will inspire confidence in you to take your finances seriously, whatever age you are, and to take personal responsibility for your financial future.

Rather than retiring in poverty, I want you to be able to afford the life you have worked hard for, during your career and during the time you've spent raising your family. Don't rely on being in a relationship with someone else providing for you; rely on yourself.

The inequalities the book explores are not deliberate. They have come about because workplace practices have been designed by men over the decades, and the financial journey that a woman follows through her life is completely different to that of a man.

This means we need to evolve our thinking and understanding, to appreciate that making things fair for women relates to so much more than just pay.

Although it still starts and ends with pay, as you will see.

I've chosen to focus on women specifically, partly because of my own experiences, but also because of the very significant impact that having children has on a woman's financial life.

But in doing my research for the book and interviewing many interesting women along the way, it's become clear that some of the issues in the workplace are not just experienced by women, but by anyone who is not a white male. We, therefore, need to identify how to evolve the culture and practices within companies, to make them genuinely inclusive.

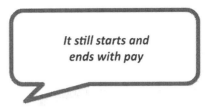

It still starts and ends with pay

Many of the ideas for improvement and change described here will benefit a broader range of employees than women alone.

Who This Book Is For

This book is a must-read for women of all ages and stages of life. It's for those of you who are:

- in your 20s and 30s, in your early career and approaching that crunch decision of starting a family
- in your 30s, 40s and 50s, who are senior managers and leaders within your company or running your own business, and well placed to initiate and lead the changes required to make your workplace fairer for women
- going through divorce or who are widowed
- turning 50, who now realise that retirement needn't be too far away if your finances are in good order
- mothers and grandmothers who want to guide your daughters and granddaughters to make better financial decisions than you did yourself

Forewarned is forearmed, and we all have the opportunity to help and support each other as women. By sharing the knowledge and ideas we have, we can inspire each other to make changes and conscious choices to improve our lives.

After reading this book, I hope you will value the goal of being financially independent and commit yourself to it.

I hope you will want to join the debate, raise awareness on social media and talk to your friends.

I hope you will feel ambitious and empowered about your value and worth, both as a mum and as a woman in the workplace, thus creating a stronger sense of your financial status.

How to Use This Book

To get the most out of the book, and to equip you to make decisions and changes, I've included some exercises, checklists and tools to use. You can download these online at:

www.dare2befair.com

Or you can use good old-fashioned pen and paper to create a personal action plan to improve your future.

Occasionally I quote facts and statistics to support what I'm saying. These are annotated with numbered references that are detailed in the Endnotes section at the back of the book.

At the end of the book are ways to contact me and keep in touch. I'd love to hear about any changes you make and the improvements you achieve. I'm always open to discussing the ideas within the book and working with you in my professional capacity as a Chartered Financial Planner.

Let's Go!

So ladies, it's time to step forward and open your eyes to the issues you may face in your financial life, and what to do about them.

Buckle up, grab the steering wheel, and be confident and ambitious.

Become a great financial decision-maker.

Help me spread the word and let's Dare To Be Fair.

CHAPTER 1

Reality Check

"A wise woman wishes to be no one's enemy; a wise woman refuses to be anyone's victim."

– Maya Angelou

In this chapter you will learn:

- how a woman's financial journey through life is typically very different to a man's
- that women are not involving themselves enough in planning for their financial future
- the financial disadvantages still facing women today
- that many contributing factors are within our control to change

---

Let's start with the shocking statistics that frame our reality today in the UK:

Women's lifetime earnings are 59% of men's[1].

This is as a result of the gender pay gap, family caring responsibilities, career breaks, part-time work and flexible hours, contributing to a 5x gender pension gap at age 65[1].

There are financial lessons for us to learn at all stages of life.

For those of you at the younger end of the age spectrum, you have more opportunities to make more changes, and so have more impact on your future life. One of the biggest take-outs from this book will, I hope, be an appreciation of the significance of your decision of how to combine work and motherhood and its long-term implications for you financially.

But equally, for those of you in mid-life or later, there are still plenty of things you can do to improve your financial position; and potentially those of others around you. You are at a stage of life where you have a lot of wisdom to share with others.

No. 1 Reality Check - Different Journeys

A woman's financial journey through life is very different to a man's. This is not solely driven by the fact that women can have children, and men can't. It's also to do with other roles that women often take on during their lives, and the choices they make at various stages.

Jane Portas, co-founder of Insuring Women's Futures, has conducted some extensive research into women's financial lives.

In her Women's Risks in Life report series she identified 12 key financial Risks in Life facing girls and women during their lifetime, which she refers to as Perils & Pitfalls. She then created 6 Moments That Matter as a way of helping girls and women think about their financial life journey to secure their financial future.

She highlights how risks sit alongside opportunities, and that the 6 Moments That Matter are points in every girl and woman's life, where the choices she makes and the support or policies available to her can have either a positive or negative effect on her long-term future. The effects are compounded in either direction so that negative impacts continue to get worse while positive impacts continue to get better over time.

They are summarised here - further information can be found at:

www.6momentsthatmatter.com

Moments That Matter[1]

1

Growing up, Studying and Requalifying.
The decisions we make about what and how we study have far-reaching consequences. The difference in women's earnings, compared to men's, is often influenced by our educational choices, and the careers they open up for us, which we then return to.

2

Entering and Re-Entering the Workplace.
Starting or returning to work is a key moment, with implications that don't only affect younger women. Role, employment, and employer choice have an impact, affecting pay and job security. Starting work, whether for the first time or later in life, is a critical time for women to establish financial independence and savings patterns.

3

Relationships, Making Up and Breaking Up.
Decisions about what form of relationship status to have, e.g. married or co-habiting, or how to share household finances can have lifelong impacts on our financial status and well-being. In particular, divorce and separation can be financially crippling for women and mothers.

4

Motherhood and Becoming a Carer.
Decisions around the time of motherhood, including sharing care and returning to work can undermine women's financial status if not fully thought through. More of us are caring for children in our 50s, while also becoming carers for older relatives, foregoing career earnings, and pension savings.

5

Later Life Planning and Entering Retirement.
Planning for later life should start early. With women having children later, caring for older relatives, living longer and spending more time as retirees, retirement planning through life and in the run-up to retirement is key. Especially as many of us are likely to have to contribute to the cost of end of life care.

> **Ill Health, Infirmity and Dying.**
> **6**   Ill health, infirmity and death impact more than the individual sufferer, they impact dependants and families too. The financial consequences of having to take time off work, change working patterns, location, or lifestyle, can be significant for our loved ones.

Figure 1. Moments That Matter

*The 6 Moments that Matter is subject to copyright and is reproduced with the kind permission of Jane Portas, extracted here from Living a financially resilient life in the UK, published by the Chartered Insurance Institute 2019. For any use or reproduction in whole or in part please seek the author's consent through **www.6momentsthatmatter. com***

These 6 Moments That Matter are key to all of us, men and women alike, allowing better understanding of the life experiences that can and are adversely affecting women's financial situations.

Men will experience these Moments too: relationship break-ups, becoming a parent, ill-health etc. However, the findings of this very extensive research show that the financial impact of these Moments is significantly worse for women than for men.

Because it can be hard to relate to other people's experiences, which we haven't personally been through, it means that men, and therefore wider society, have not yet fully acknowledged these differences.

Currently, there is limited appreciation of the short-term and longer-term impacts these Moments can have on women's lives —their mindset, their ambitions and their financial security.

This phenomenon is known as unconscious male bias. It needs to be acknowledged and understood before it can be addressed.

A great example of how this bias can show itself, even with the best of intentions, is explained by Caroline Criado Perez in her fascinating book, Invisible Women: Exposing Data Bias in a World Designed for Men.

In 2011 the town of Karlskoga, Sweden followed the procedures of most administrations when it came to clearing snow. It began with the major traffic routes and ended with pedestrian walkways and bicycle paths. But this was affecting men and women in different ways because men and women travel differently. The town council didn't have separate travel data for men and women, so the male policymakers were using their own experience and judgement to decide the order of priority for snow-clearing.

Not only were men and women using different modes of transport, their reasons for travelling were also often different too. For example, men were more likely to be commuting into and out of the city centre twice a day, whereas women were more likely to be doing a school run before going to work themselves, or going to care for an elderly relative, meaning that their journeys were more complex across and around the city.

Having become aware of this, the town councillors switched their snow clearing schedule to prioritise pedestrian walkways and public transport users; and ended up with an unanticipated benefit. The number of hospital admissions for women suffering injuries in slippery and icy conditions fell dramatically, saving the town money overall. The cost of accidents was much greater than the winter clearing schedule for the town.

This is a simple but interesting example of how things we might take for granted, and the logic behind them e.g. clearing roads first to ensure people can get to work and continue their economic activity, are reflective of what men do, as opposed to what is true for women or a broader section of society.

Similarly, workplace practices, legislation and social policy have evolved driven and influenced mainly from the perspective of a man's financial life journey and reflect the typical male career path.

It's not surprising therefore that these key moments in a woman's life, specifically her financial life, have been missed or undervalued. Addressing these Moments That Matter will fundamentally improve women's financial futures and financial security.

If you would like to learn more about the 6 Moments That Matter where you can download a Financial Wellbeing Guide, go to:

www.6momentsthatmatter.com

No. 2 Reality Check - There May Not Be a Prince Charming

Women don't involve themselves in long-term financial planning in the same way that men do and this needs to change.

Many reasons sit behind this reality: if women are not the main breadwinners, they can default to gender stereotypes and believe that their partner will take care of them financially and provide for them, not only now but also in the future.

Merryn Somerset Webb, the editor of the Financial Times Money section, has written a book called Love Is Not Enough. In it, she confesses that despite being a self-sufficient and independent woman, somewhere in the back of her mind, she used to assume that in later life there would be a man who would provide for her.

This is the "happy ever after" princess narrative we grew up with – "one day our Prince will come."

Disney has a lot to answer for. However, it's interesting to see how Disney has been changing their female narrative over the last twenty years. Their more recent films feature very different female characters to Cinderella, Sleeping Beauty, Snow White or Belle in Beauty and the Beast. Having dabbled with warrior-like female leads such as Mulan and Pocahontas, they have settled for more relatable but equally strong and independent female leads: Moana, Tiana and Elsa.

Childhood and historical narratives are incredibly powerful influences on our unconscious mind. I look at this in the next chapter, as they shape our mindset and can create limiting beliefs.

By being aware of them, we can change our narrative into something healthier and more constructive for our future benefit.

If we unconsciously believe that someone else is going to provide for us in our later life, this may hold us back from striving to be financially self-sufficient in our own right.

No. 3 Reality Check - Bad Things Happen

When we enter a long-term relationship and get married, we usually cannot imagine that we might separate or divorce. But the reality is that 43%, more than four in ten marriages in England and Wales, end in divorce[2].

Given that statistic, should we be relying on anyone other than ourselves for our financial security?

If you picture yourself in retirement with a loving partner by your side, that is to be hoped for, but the statistics are telling a different story.

The average age for divorce in the UK is just under 44 for women and 46.4 for men, and the age group of 45-49 years has the highest divorce rate. However, the rate of divorce is rising fastest amongst the so-called silver splitters, those over 60[2].

The third reality check here is that many financial settlements, agreed when divorcing, fail to adequately take into account the longer-term situation for the lower earner in the relationship, normally the woman.

It can be a similar situation if you experience unexpected or early bereavement. We might never imagine that our partner will not be there with us tomorrow. But unfortunately, life can throw some very unwelcome and nasty curveballs our way, and if you think about your network of friends and family, you probably all know some-one whose life has been significantly affected by death or serious ill-health. We just never think it will happen to us.

Facing such personal crises is not the best time to be trying to understand your financial situation for the very first time.

I will talk in Chapter 4 about how to prepare yourself in advance of these potentially difficult and emotional times.

No. 4 Reality Check - The Gender Pay Gap Still Exists

The gender pay gap is shrinking but still stands at 15.5% if you are in your 30s[3].

The underlying factors that cause a difference in pay are clearly complex and are a combination of individual choices and behaviours, as well as institutionalised workplace culture and practices — nothing that can't be changed or adjusted, however. If there is buy-in to the need for change, then the will and motivation will be created to make change happen.

There is one particular inflection point that can change the trajectory of a woman's financial future and plays into the gender pay gap significantly: the decisions women make about their career and combining career with motherhood. Most of us have no idea of the long-term financial consequences of the decisions we make at this stage of our lives.

It's such an important issue, one that we have a huge amount of personal influence over, that I've dedicated a whole chapter to it.

We usually never consider the full facts, because it's hard to calculate the potential financial impact of the choices we make on our lives in 20 or 30 years' time. But we need this information to be able to make the best-informed decisions about maternity leave, career breaks, and whether or how we return to work.

These decisions not only deeply affect our financial future but also our mindset, our sense of value and self-worth. This subject is very close to my heart and is one that should be high up on the agenda for all women who want to be in the 'driving seat' of their own life.

Over the last 30 years, supported by the extension of statutory maternity pay, it seems to have become the 'norm' for mums to return to work part-time rather than full-time, after having a baby.

Whilst I appreciate it is a positive change in many ways for women to have this choice, it is a double-edged sword. The effect it has on a woman's pay and pension over the long term is dramatic.

Workplace culture and practices feed into the complex causes behind the gender pay gap but there are many ways of making positive changes that can make things fairer for women and particularly for working mums.

Location, working hours, how skills are assessed, how pay and promotions are awarded – these are all explored in detail within the book.

I hope there will be an upward challenge from the younger generations in the workplace, but the current generation of senior managers in their 30s, 40s and older have a responsibility, as well as the opportunity, to accelerate change in their organisations.

There Is Hope and Opportunity

All of these reality checks are leading to serious financial disadvantages for women. Worryingly, it is often only at the point of retirement, divorce, or death of a partner, that they hit home.

This book aims to highlight the issues and propose practical changes and steps we can take to reduce the financial disadvantages so that women do not have to face poverty or a lower standard of living in later life.

Imagine you work hard all your life, whether employed, running your own business, raising children and running the household, juggling work and family commitments, caring for elderly relatives.

How devastating it is then to reach an age when you want to stop working, only to realise that you cannot afford to; that you simply don't have enough financial resources to maintain your standard of living in your retirement, without working.

And if this situation has been created because of the choices you made with your partner at the time of having children, how can this be fair?

Men have a critical role to play in making life financially fairer for women — in the way they support their wives and their daughters at a personal level, in the workplace and in society.

We can strive to be financially self-sufficient at all stages of our life, but it's particularly needed in later life. We don't know if we will be living on our own or be in a relationship. We may not yet know whether we will have children or not.

This is why this book is relevant for women of all ages. As a 52-year-old myself, with a son of 23 and a daughter of 12, I want to be part of the change that makes their futures much fairer for women in society and the workplace.

Now we have a shared context for some of the challenges still facing women in the 2020s, let's explore the opportunities for change and how we can Dare To Be Fair.

CHAPTER 2

Women's Money Mindset

"You don't become what you want, you become what you believe."

- Oprah Winfrey

> *In this chapter you will learn:*
>
> - how your childhood influences may have created limiting beliefs about money
> - that your partner's money mindset may be very different to your own
> - how the money narrative over the last 60 years is slowly changing
> - how this may be contributing to your sense of worth and value in the workplace

I'm sure it won't surprise you to hear that, generally speaking, men and women have a different relationship with money, particularly regarding being paid what they think they are worth. This chapter will help you explore and better understand your relationship with money. I have never been driven by money as my main motivation for fulfilment or self-worth. For me, having enough money enables me to be independent, self-sufficient, and make my own choices.

What is 'enough'? This is a very interesting question and is certainly something you should spend time thinking about.

In Morgan Housel's book The Psychology of Money: Timeless lessons on wealth, greed and happiness, he re-tells an anecdote:

> At a party given by a billionaire on Shelter Island, Kurt Vonnengut informs his pal, Joseph Keller, that their host, a hedge fund manager, had made more money in a single day than Heller had earned from his wildly popular novel Catch-22 over its whole history.
>
> Heller responds, "Yes, but I have something he will never have....enough."

I encourage you to think about what "enough" means for you, as you start to create your financial plan for the future.

I am no psychologist, and the content of this chapter is drawn from the insights of professionals with knowledge in this area, as well as from my experiences as a keen people watcher and observer of behaviour.

My work as a financial planner affords me insights into how people think about money, how it impacts their sense of value and worth and whether they have a healthy outlook on their finances. Understanding this enables me to support and guide them to a point where they feel more in control of their money and their future. For those who are already in a good place, I help them take the next steps to feel empowered and confident in their own ability to be a great financial decision-maker.

Looking Back: Childhood Influences

Our views, beliefs and values about money today were shaped in our childhood by our family and the people we grew up with. It was what we heard, saw and inferred during that period of our life that has created our belief system. This may be a positive system, or there may be some limiting beliefs within it. During our childhood, we learn how important money is or isn't in our daily lives.

There can be a big difference growing up in a household where money is not a problem, compared to a household where it's often a struggle to pay the bills and your parents are always arguing about money. And how your parents dealt with money will have been influenced by their parents.

As our relationship with money is usually formed from our childhood experiences, I will share mine with you now. Growing up, we relied solely on my father's earnings. My mother and father took on very traditional roles within the family. My mother trained as a nurse and worked at Great Ormond Street in her early 20s, and when she had me at the age of 25, she gave up work and never went back or did any paid work again. My father had a good job at Lloyds Bank and worked in London for most of his career, before moving to a different role and company in his 50s, working three days a week (which was quite radical and unusual at the time).

My impression is that we lived a comfortable life and we escaped any real concerns or issues associated with not having enough money. When I think back, I'm amazed that my father's earnings managed to stretch as far as they did, but in those days, the cost of a house and a mortgage relative to your earnings were much lower than today. It was perfectly possible to afford a mortgage based on one person's salary alone.

My strongest recollection of how this played out for us as children, was where we went on holiday each summer. At the age of six, one of my earliest memories is going abroad for the first time. We had a two-week holiday in Majorca and flew out on my brother's fourth birthday. This started a pattern in which, every other year we would return to the same resort in Majorca for two weeks, and in the interim years, we would go to Clacton and stay in my Nan's caravan for a week or two to economise. Both holidays gave us equal joy and pleasure — genuinely. As much as I loved the beaches and blue sea of Majorca, I have very fond memories of waking up in the top bunk in the caravan, listening to the squirrels running along the roof, and the sound of wood pigeons cooing.

We didn't spend much money on clothes — a lot of mine came courtesy of my cousin Samantha, who was 3 years older than me — and we never ate out in restaurants. The odd fish & chip takeaway was always a rare treat.

My parents, who were born during the Second World War and grew up in the 1950s and '60s, had 'moved on' socially and financially compared to their parents, moving out of north London, buying their own house and settling in Essex. I think it was always their expectation and hope that their children would continue that trend, with education and hard work being their mantras of success.

I wasn't encouraged to have a Saturday job when I was at school, as education and therefore homework was considered the number one priority.

My first experience of managing my own money was when I went to university.

I worked through the long summer holiday, managing to earn enough money to support myself during term time. I came out of that experience very much a saver, being conservative with how I spent my money and had developed some basic skills in planning. This was as simple as recognising that sometimes I had to go without right then, to afford something better or something I really wanted in the future. The classic example was, that to afford a ticket to the May Ball, I had to cut back on my pints of cider in the bar, to save money in the weeks before the tickets went on sale.

In my work as a qualified Financial Planner, I talk to all my clients about this requirement to make a short-term sacrifice now, for the prospect of achieving a bigger future gain — this is the essence of investing and building wealth.

The money my father earned was carefully spent, and he certainly instilled in me the importance of saving and living within your means. In my professional work now, I see very clearly that people generally fall into one of two categories: they are either a Saver or a Spender, by nature.

Which one are you?

And if you are in a long-term relationship, is your partner the same as you or the opposite?

The fascinating thing I have now observed with my children is that this instinctive preference shows itself at a very young age — one is a spender, the other a saver — so maybe this is just as much about nature as nurture?

I am instinctively a Saver and the principle of "living within my means" has continued throughout my life. During my 20s and 30s, I would say I was

Are you a Saver or a Spender?

quite tight with my money and my spending. This only changed when, after my first marriage had ended and I was living as a single mum, working full-time, I realised that for years I had hardly ever spent money on myself.

Fortunately, I soon figured out that I *am* worth spending my own money on and now have a much healthier mindset about money and how I value myself.

Limiting Beliefs

This leads us nicely into the topic of how our limiting beliefs can affect the way we think and the relationship we have with money. We absorb these beliefs throughout our childhood, and they sit in our unconscious mind, influencing the way we think and behave.

According to Katherine Hurst, writer on TheLawOfAttraction.com, the following are examples of limiting beliefs that relate to money:

1. **Believing You Don't Deserve Money**

   If you grew up believing that money was something that other people had, or that you didn't have enough money to afford to do the things you wanted, then you might translate that into believing that you don't deserve money and nice things. As a result, even the thought of having enough money is not something you are striving to achieve in adulthood.

2. **Having Negative or Scary Thoughts about Money**

   These can often come from a childhood experience in which there was not enough money to go around, therefore the thought of not having enough money is something that feels scary. It can be a real money block to you, striving to have more money now than you did when you were growing up.

3. **Being Overly Generous with Money**

   Whilst generosity is good, it should not be to the point where you're impacting your circumstances because of it, by not leaving yourself with enough money to spend on yourself.

4. **Fear of Success or Achievement**

   Your subconscious mind may be terrified of getting what it wants and be blocking you without you realising it. This can lead to you rationalising to yourself that you don't need or want to earn a lot of money.

If you grew up in a household where money was no issue and you could have whatever you wanted, within reason, you may end up with a princess mentality, thinking that someone else will always provide for you.

However, I've also seen the opposite outcome with clients of mine. Some who grew up very aware that they had a wealthy or privileged background are now more determined to make their own way in the world, and not to rely on their parents.

Exercise:

I encourage you to analyse your own situation. Use the following exercise to record what you remember about your childhood in terms of money; how you felt about it then and feel about it now; what you witnessed about your parents' relationship with money; and how this may have influenced your current thinking and relationship with money.

The way in which we can stop these limiting beliefs getting in the way of our success, holding us back, or feeling artificially 'provided for', is first to acknowledge them; then, to work at ways of minimising them.

1. What did your parents teach you about money?
2. What do you think you learned about money from them as you were growing up?
3. Did they try to 'keep up with the Joneses'?
4. Did they struggle to make ends meet?
5. Were they comfortable talking about money, or was it a very private matter?
6. Did your mum work and earn her own money?
7. Who held the purse strings?
8. Did they have a lot of debt?
9. Did they pay their bills on time?
10. Were they organised or disorganised with money?

Download this exercise at: www.dare2befair.com

Have a think about the answers to these questions and then consider: can you see your parents' beliefs and values about money in yourself?

How similar or dissimilar to them are you? Is this a good thing or a bad thing?

How does it translate into your relationship with money now?

- Do you live within or beyond your means?
- Do you rely on debt to make ends meet each month?
- Are you quite comfortable and careful with your money?

If you are in a long-term relationship, it's important to talk to your partner about their experiences too. Ask them to go through this same exercise, so that they can reflect on the belief system that their parents have instilled in them, and how it translates into their current relationship with money.

Spend an evening discussing your different experiences. See where you are similar and where you are different.

I guarantee it will result in a much deeper understanding of each other, as our relationship with money and our attitude to it, is such an important part of life.

It may help you explain or identify certain things about yourself and each other — and don't ignore any red flags it might raise either. If you are a saver and your partner is a spender, then maybe you need to be running the bank accounts, the household finances and the investments, if you're not already.

You're then both in a much more informed position to talk about where your values are similar to each other, and where you differ. These things are important when it comes to your joint financial planning. They will influence your perspective on, for example, whether to support your children financially once they are 18 or young adults.

I have worked with some couples who have divergent views on this, with one parent wanting to support their children financially as much as they possibly can afford to do, and the other feeling more inclined to let them stand on their own two feet. These differing views are likely to come from your different belief systems.

As with all areas of parenting, you may have different preferences and approaches on how to bring up your children, so don't forget the financial side of life.

Remember too that you will be influencing *their* future relationship with money.

Setting a positive example by talking openly about money within the family is a great thing to do, creating a healthy and open relationship with your finances. You can align on what's important for the short, medium and long-term and become a confident financial decision-maker for yourself and jointly, within your relationship.

Being Grown Up

Taking financial responsibility for ourselves requires a grown-up mindset. I can clearly remember the time when I first felt financially grown up: when I signed the papers for my first joint mortgage at the age of 25. The fact that a bank was prepared to lend us so much money and that it was now our responsibility to pay it back, was quite a moment.

Many people use this phrase when they first take financial advice and like the plan they have in front of them. Whether it's finally understanding their pensions and planning pro-actively with a goal in mind for their future income, or whether it's finally investing the cash they have been diligently saving but not making the most of in their savings account.

They will often turn to me and say with a grin "wow, I feel like a grown-up!" It's a very positive feeling, as it means they feel empowered and in control, which leads to a greater sense of contentment for them.

However, some people resist growing up. This is known as Peter Pan syndrome. Someone who dabbles in relationships and doesn't commit, can sometimes behave badly and selfishly like a child, and who continually prioritises short-term needs over the longer term.

Journalist Tracy Macmillan, writing for the online *Huffpost*, has observed this in many women, and calls it Princess Pan, the female Peter Pan. There is a desire to stay young, to dress in skinny jeans and deny the fact you're getting older, including taking responsibility for your financial future.

This can lead to something I often observe – being an ostrich and keeping your head stuck in the sand. This can continue until middle age (typically turning 50) or until something in your life forces you to raise your head and acknowledge that you need to get your finances under control. It doesn't necessarily mean your finances are in a bad place — although, for some, this is, unfortunately, the case. But it's a long overdue wake-up call to start getting your life in order.

The Money Narrative Through History

The next thing we need to explore is how society thinks about women and money, how we have got to our current point in time, and how the narrative has developed over the last 50 to 60 years.

I was stunned to realise how relatively recently some changes for women took place, as I took for granted some of the things that are the norm today.

There's no doubt that the historical narrative, the things we heard when we were growing up, the things we read about in newspapers and magazines given to us by our parents and grandparents is hugely significant and influential.

Society's attitudes can take generations to evolve and change, so in some ways, the pace of change for women's emancipation concerning money has been remarkable over the last 50 years. With the right constructive pressure, this change can be accelerated, as we have witnessed recently with #blacklivesmatter and #metoo, which hopefully will lead to lasting and permanent change for the better.

Let's start with the influence of the Second World War. At that time, when the men were away fighting, women took over the work and the jobs that the men had previously done and were earning the money. This was an emergency at the time, but one that extended through the post-war decade. Many women remained in the workplace, often through necessity to earn enough to live on, rather than because of job satisfaction. There were severe food rations for many years and a scarcity of many day-to-day items that we take for granted, and so money was needed purely to survive.

Money was tight for the vast majority of people — a true period of austerity, which lasted for most of the next decade. So this experience for our parents and grandparents was significant. If they grew up in the immediate aftermath of the war, they will probably have grown up living with a scarcity of food at various points in their life and not being able to afford so much of what we now consider to be basic and essential, and what they thought of as a luxury.

The age of consumerism had not yet started. Household appliances were basic and not automated, with most families not being able to afford to own electrical goods – Radio Rentals existed to rent out radios, televisions and eventually video recorders. Central heating with radiators was not widely available in most houses through the 1950s and 1960s, it only really became affordable in the 1970s. Similarly, telephones were only affordable for the well-off; in 1970 only 35% of UK homes had a telephone[1].

The other thing to consider, which has hugely influenced whether women work or not, is the provision of childcare. Most childcare in those days was informal, provided by family members and friends, enabling the woman to take on part-time work to earn some additional money. J   ever, the man was the main breadwinner who worked full ti   - a "woman's place was in the home."

It's therefore cle   o see how the narrative of how the man was the one who conc   ed himself with the money and the finances came about. *Whoe   arns the money controls the money.*

This still holds for many families today. The potential negative consequence of this is that *whoever controls the money controls the relationship*, for good or for bad — more of this in Chapter 4.

> *Whoever controls the money, controls the relationship*

By the 1970s, the women's movement had made great strides, with the availability of the contraceptive pill in the 1960s creating a fundamental shift in a woman's ability to control her own life. However, if you were a married woman, you could only have a bank account in joint names with your husband, not in your sole name. This meant that the man had to sign off on any financial transactions, so the wife had no autonomy. That was only 50 years ago.

If you were a single woman at that time, you could have a personal bank account, so the narrative here was that once a woman was married, the husband controlled the purse strings.

He was the provider, the one whose wage was intended to cover all the family's needs with the woman not needing to contribute financially. Therefore he was the one who made the big financial decisions; the inference being that women weren't capable of making financial decisions if they were not working.

What flawed logic. But actually, to what extent do you think this narrative persists today?

My experience shows me that many women have absorbed this narrative and reflect this mindset within their relationship when it comes to making long-term decisions.

It's clear that then, as today, women usually do hold the purse-strings for immediate and short-term purchases, particularly when it comes to groceries, shopping, and anything to do with running the household and providing for the children.

In my mum's day, she was given her weekly housekeeping money by my dad. She, like all women, learned to budget and spend very carefully in those days. She had to stick within the housekeeping allowance, and it would not have been acceptable to over-spend. This mentality enabled women to develop strong skills in short-term budgeting, planning, and making smart priority decisions about what was needed and what they could do without.

Over the years, as the level of disposable income has grown, the price of consumer goods has come down, and access to credit has become easier, these skills have been an easy habit to fall out of, but it's still probably *the* most important financial planning principle – don't spend what you haven't got!

Don't spend what you haven't got!

The Money Narrative Today

In these modern times, I believe the narrative is slowly changing.

Whilst many women are making joint decisions with their partner about family life over the next few years, I observe however that it is less common for women to be fully involved in longer-term family decisions; for example, how to support their children through University, or whether to save or invest to provide their children with money for a house deposit. These long-term decisions about supporting your children are best made as soon as they are born, giving you as much time as possible to put money aside.

Even less common, whether you're in a relationship or single, is time spent thinking about your retirement and later life: what it looks like, when it should start, how much money you will need and whether you're likely to have enough. In my experience, it is still quite unlikely that the woman is the instigator of these conversations. It probably links back to the historical narrative, that if the man is the main provider, then it's the man who has the responsibility for these decisions.

What do you think about that? Do you recognise that you default to your partner for long-term financial decisions? Have you ever thought and talked about your life 10 years from now?

Do you assume that your partner has superior knowledge about this that you don't? Let me assure you, even if he works in the financial services industry, it doesn't automatically equip him with a full understanding of pensions and investments, even though he may be more comfortable with money and numbers. As alluded to, depending on his relationship with money, he may not be the best one of you in the relationship to be taking on that responsibility.

If you know your partner spends more than you do, or you know he is not good with money then you should be stepping in and changing those roles and responsibilities.

Alternatively, are you the main breadwinner in your relationship? And do you, as a result of this, take the lead with the financial decision-making, sorting out the mortgage and planning for the future, rather than leaving it your partner?

Exercise:

As an exercise, reflect on your own situation and compare it to what you know about your close friends or other family members.

Be fully conscious of your own situation and consider – as you read the rest of the book – whether you are happy with it or whether you want to change it.

- List the positive female role models that you know in your life, and what it is you love about them.

- Do you know any women who are the main breadwinners within the family?

- Do you think that translates into a different decision-making framework for that family?

- Is that something that you would like to emulate?

- If you are taking the lead with your finances – whether on your own or in a relationship – how far ahead are you planning?

It's likely the younger generation will have a slightly different money mindset to those of us in middle age or older. The narrative has hopefully progressed to a point where they consider men and women to have much more equal financial status in a relationship (although they will have been influenced by us as their parents).

As women are becoming increasingly successful at school, university and in the workplace, their earnings potential is stronger than it has ever been.

If you are in your 20s or 30s and are in a relationship, are both of you earning at similar levels?

If one is earning more than the other, has that changed how you both discuss money and make financial decisions together?

How Women Value Themselves in the Workplace

A key area relating to women's money mindsets is how we perceive our value and self-worth, how this translates into our behaviour in the workplace and ultimately what we earn and how we manage our career.

There has been a lot written about the fact that women typically undervalue their skills and experience, compared to men. It is hard-wired into us from childhood to be modest about our achievements and successes, as no one likes a bragger. But when the accepted rules are different for men, the playing field is no longer level or fair.

You may be aware of the well-researched scenario of a man and woman, equally well qualified, considering a job application. If the man can tick three or four of the 10 boxes of skills and experience required, he will apply for the job. However, the woman will only apply if she feels she can tick eight, nine or even 10 of the boxes because she has some doubts over her ability to do the job – the classic imposter syndrome.

This different perception of competency, and belief in being able to perform a role to a high standard, affects how men and women evaluate their individual skills and relevance for jobs. It has a very strong impact on the frequency and type of promotions that women put themselves forward for.

As a self-confessed perfectionist, I have a Post-It note on my screen to remind me: strive for excellence, not perfection.

Assessing our self-worth against an impossible ideal of perfection is damaging over time. On the other hand, a healthy and strong sense of self-worth gives us inner security, meaning we can rely on ourselves rather than turning to others.

> *Strive for Excellence, not Perfection*

Salary and earnings are often said to be a stronger motivator for men than for women in their careers. However, research by Lluminari Inc, a U.S. health and wellness company, concluded that men and women value the same things in the workplace, just with different emphases.

Male workers regard pay, benefits, authority, status and power noticeably more than female workers. Women place their greatest workplace values on relationships, respect, communication, fairness, equity, collaboration and work-family balance. Interestingly, men do not tend to be especially aware of the factors that women value and women tend to overestimate how much men value money, status and power.

From the perspective of senior female leaders I speak to, they say it is often the grade or the title of a role that motivates women more than the actual pay itself.

But one should be inseparable from the other as far as the employer is concerned. Awarding an increased grade should be matched by an appropriate increase in pay, regardless of whether the person is expecting it, or indeed demanding it. More about fair remuneration in Chapter 6.

The assessment of personal value in the workplace is not necessarily something that just affects women. In my conversations with senior leaders, it's clear that the same challenge is often experienced by individuals who are in an ethnic minority group or who are disabled. It is a much wider issue, affecting anyone who is not the stereotypical white male.

Risk Aware, Not Risk Averse

Finally, as we consider women's money mindsets, it's often said that women are more cautious, or more risk-averse than men when managing money or investing. It is well documented that women will typically have more money held as cash and less of it invested than men.

When it comes to managing money, the female role of nurturing and raising children means that she has to ensure there is enough food to go around and that the money available will last (back to managing the housekeeping budget). She therefore may be less inclined to take a risk with money.

This can show itself as a conscious or unconscious characteristic in women. I would better summarise it by saying that women are more risk aware than men, rather than risk averse: they may evaluate things as a risk that men do not.

Interestingly, this can lead to women being more successful investors than men, over the medium to long-term, as evidenced in studies conducted by Warwick Business School amongst 2,800 men and women, and Hargreaves Lansdown, the UK's largest consumer investment platform[2].

It means that women are often best placed to be the main financial decision-maker for the benefit of the family's long-term future.

One thing I want to squash is the idea that just because a man may be the main breadwinner and may occasionally skim through the money pages of the weekend newspaper that it qualifies him with more knowledge or a better understanding of financial planning or investing than it does a woman.

> *Women are often best-placed to be the main financial decision-maker*

In fact, in my experience, a pressure often felt by men is they feel they should understand more about money and investing than they do. They may be afraid to reveal that they don't necessarily have all the answers when it comes to understanding pensions, or knowing how best to invest, whether this is in front of work colleagues, mates down the pub or in the eyes of their wife.

Your partner may not acknowledge or admit this of course, and this is where you can play a strong role in the relationship, by encouraging joint decision-making with the finances and encouraging more open conversation about future financial goals and priorities.

Front and Centre

I hope this exploration of women's money mindsets has been thought-provoking and has enabled you to better understand yourself, your partner, and your respective relationships with money.

The important thing is what you do with that deeper insight now you better understand what's influencing you.

My key focus for you is in two specific areas:

- How do you view and assess your financial worth in the workplace?
- How do you view and assess your financial worth within your relationship?

I want to overturn the limiting belief that the main breadwinner – the man – has to call all the financial shots. He should not hold the purse strings for the 'bigger, more important' longer-term financial decisions. I assume that you are fully involved in, if not leading, the decision-making on the day-to-day finances, and all I encourage you to do now is to extend your influence into the medium and longer term.

It is important to develop a shared financial responsibility in your partnership. Putting yourself front and centre in managing your finances and planning for the future will help protect you from the unexpected and provide a shared sense of control.

The following chapters will explain more about how central this is to achieving financial fairness in your personal life. They will equip you with enough knowledge to start straight away.

Having more confidence about your financial situation can create greater self-confidence in the workplace and in managing your career. You can fully appreciate your value and worth to your employer, knowing the importance of the money you earn and how it benefits you and your family.

CHAPTER 3

Personal Financial Planning

"Money makes the world go round."

**– Liza Minelli as Sally Bowles
in Cabaret.**

In this chapter you will learn:

- the basic principles of good financial planning
- how to assess your current situation
- what the financial jargon means
- the wonder of compounding and how it works
- what to be aware of when investing for the future

Planning Your Future

Whether you are single or in a relationship, how often do you think about and plan for the longer term? It's something that we as humans find quite hard to do naturally, some people more than others.

You may be in a relationship where you feel you have a good level of balance and collaboration in your joint decision-making. This is great, although ask yourself whether most of the decisions you make together are focused on the short term, which in my financial planning world means the next 5 years.

Are you putting money aside? Are you investing for your own or your family's benefit in the future and considering your potential financial needs, for example, in 10 years' time?

Do you want to send your children to a private school in future? Do you want to save on their behalf, so they can buy a car when they pass their test?

Have you ever talked about retirement with your partner and discussed what that looks like for both of you? Do you agree on what age you are aiming for?

What will you do if your parents need to pay for care? Will you step in and help?

Some of these conversations are likely to become more top of mind as you get older. There's certainly a switch that flicks on when you turn 50 that brings into focus the prospect of retiring. By that point, it will feel a lot more within reach, and therefore something that you want to think about and plan for.

I hope to demonstrate, investing sufficiently to ensure you have enough money to live on when you stop working is *the* number one long-term priority you should be addressing much earlier in your life, ideally in your 30s and 40s.

Who Wears the Trousers?

Talking about money with your partner is *so* important to build an equal and fair relationship, which has solid financial foundations, to provide security and peace of mind for both of you.

Secrecy and lack of transparency can lead to issues. The Money Advice Service has found that 13% of UK adults have a stash of money hidden from their partner and that the average couple has 39 arguments about money per year[1]. We know that a lack of money and worry over debt can be a huge strain for us as individuals and within a relationship.

If you live with your partner, you probably have shared responsibilities within the household and relationship and also some separate ones, such as 'blue jobs' and 'pink jobs.'

That's certainly true in my relationship — I'm not wheeling the bins out on a Tuesday night, that's his job!

But joking aside, the key thing to appreciate is that when it comes to money, whoever has control of the finances, really has control of the relationship. This can, unfortunately, lead to a misuse of control in some relationships, resulting in coercion and abuse which must be called out and addressed.

But even in the best of relationships, it means that you need to be fully involved in the long-term as well as the short-term decision-making within your relationship, in order to influence and control your future.

Start With the End in Mind

How can we prioritise what we want to spend our money on in the short, medium and longer-term?

What's important to us changes at different stages of our lives. When we are first starting out as young adults in our 20s, most of our earnings will likely be spent paying rent, or a mortgage, paying the bills and general living costs. You may be saving for a house deposit if you are renting or still living at home. You may be saving to get married. There may not be much left over each month.

And yet somehow, are you still able to afford a daily expensive coffee from a coffee shop? Are you buying lunch at work rather than taking food into the office with you from home? You may still be able to afford a drink most evenings after work, subscriptions to your favourite channels or tickets to see your favourite bands or artists. (This is not limited to 20-year-olds only, of course.)

And whilst we all want to live and enjoy life, we need to be conscious that by prioritising our short-term needs and spending all the money we have, we are missing out on the opportunity to invest some of this money for even greater rewards or benefits in future.

In this fast-paced age of intense consumerism, it can feel difficult to defer the immediate enjoyment of our money for something more intangible in years to come.

And yet if something is really important to you — like planning a fantastic holiday, paying for a wedding or a house deposit — then we generally find it easier to save money towards it. The point being, we are able to value a future goal when it is tangible, and sometimes find it harder to save or invest with no specific goal in mind. The key to success, therefore, is to think about your future goals, articulate them, define them, and then prioritise them.

If you continue to live comfortably in the present and do not make any provision for your longer-term future, you may regret it in later life.

I had a very clear example of this when I was recently working with some clients. One of the first things the wife said to me when I asked what amount of savings they had was "well, no one really saves much these days, do they?"

They wanted me to review their pensions and confirm when they would have enough income to stop working. I had to break the news to them that they would *never* have enough income from their pensions to fund their current lifestyle.

Because they had lived their lives "not being good with money" in their words, prioritising the present and spending all their money as they went, they would have to make big changes and sacrifices in 5 years when they planned to stop working. These included: selling their house and moving out of the area they had lived in for 30 years, to buy somewhere cheaper, carrying on working for another 5-10 years, or just not having any money left to eat out or go out for a drink each week after paying the bills.

They thought that not saving or investing was the norm, but most people I work with do recognise the importance of investing their surplus income each month, for that future nest egg or rainy day.

So, to avoid that situation yourself, it's best to think through your priorities and define your short, medium and longer-term goals. If you are in a relationship, you should discuss and agree on these with your partner.

It's fine to have an open-ended investment with no particular timeframe or goal in mind, but in my experience, it's far easier to stick to the plan and keep on track if your goals are specific.

It's far easier to stick to the plan if your goals are specific

It makes them more real, and it stops you from straying or being tempted to skip a month of contributions just because you've seen the most amazing pair of shoes, handbag, band tickets etc., which you can't live without.

This is what your cash savings or emergency funds are for; so that you don't derail your longer-term planning. Ideally, you should always have about 3 months' expenditure in cash savings, which you can access quickly.

Examples of medium to long-term goals could be:

- planning to take a year off work in five years' time to go travelling
- celebrating a future birthday or wedding anniversary with a party (big parties don't come cheap these days)
- supporting your children's education through private school
- buying your 17-year-old their first car
- helping your children with a house deposit, when they are in their mid to late 20s (we've all heard a lot in the media about the Bank of Mum and Dad being in the top ten of the UK's largest lenders)
- buying a holiday home in the UK or abroad
- having the financial resources to stop earning by the time you are 60, to do volunteer work
- saving a fund for the grandchildren

Identifying and planning for a few key goals is something I encourage you to do, and it's something I do with my clients right from the first meeting.

Where Are You Now?

There are two key steps in creating a successful financial plan:

Step 1.   Identify those future goals and priorities that are fundamentally important to you.

- This will enable you to live the life you want to live.

Step 2.   Understand your current situation.

- Track your income and your expenditure and ensure you are living within your means.

- Clear any expensive debt, such as credit cards or anything that is not on a structured repayment plan, such as a mortgage or car finance.
- Build your cash savings to act as emergency funds.

Here are some tools to help you evaluate your current situation, and to assess how in control of your financial situation you are right now.

Income and Expenditure Summary Sheet

ANNUAL INCOME	PERSON 1	PERSON 2	TOTAL
Gross Annual Salary			
Pension			
Annual bonus (avg)			
TOTAL			
MONTHLY INCOME			
Earned Income – net			
Salary – net			
Other			
Earnings			
Unearned Income			
Rental Property			
Pension Income			
State Benefits			
Investment Income			
Child Maintenance			
Other			
Earnings			
TOTAL			

MONTHLY EXPENDITURE		TOTAL
ESSENTIAL		
Mortgage / rent		
Council Tax		
Water / utilities		
TOTAL		
INSURANCE POLICIES		
Buildings & Contents		
Car		
Life Assurance		
Private / medical		
Critical illness		
Income Protection		
TOTAL		
DISCRETIONARY		
Food & Drink – home		
Food & Drink – out		
Car expenses		
Clothing		
Package / leisure memberships		
School fees		
TV / broadband / mobile		
Online subscriptions		
Gym membership		
Leisure		
Holidays		
Loan / debt repayments		
Monthly savings		
TOTAL		

Surplus / deficit		0
GRAND TOTAL		

Figure 2. Income and Expenditure Summary Sheet

Download the above spreadsheet at: www.dare2befair.com

This is a simple spreadsheet, one that I send to all my prospective clients to complete before our first meeting. On the left, it captures your annual income — your gross annual salary or earnings, any rental income you receive, any significant investment income you receive

— and then it looks at your net monthly income. Net means after tax and national insurance (NI) contributions have been deducted; gross is the value before tax and NI have been deducted.

This can be summarised for each individual in the family who has income.

Then on the right, a summary of your monthly expenditure, classified as essential i.e. committed spend, usually mortgage/rent, council tax, bills, cost of travelling to work and insurance; and discretionary i.e. spend that you have some ability to influence, vary or decide not to lay out.

This spreadsheet is very basic, and you can find more detailed options on the internet, but I believe this is sufficient to capture 90% at least of your monthly and annual spend. With some expenditure such as clothes and holidays, which you may not normally think of in terms of monthly spend, just work out your spend in a typical year and divide by 12.

The spreadsheet also prompts you to capture any monthly loan repayments, as well as monthly savings or investments.

If your total income exceeds your total expenditure, you are in a good position, you are living within your means. Although your expenditure may vary from month to month, if it is 90% or less than your income, then you should feel that you are in balance each month.

If the amount of surplus calculated by the spreadsheet doesn't look right to you and seems too high, it means you're spending far more on your discretionary items than you realise.

Going through your bank statements is a good idea at this stage, maybe the last six months, to build up a more accurate picture of your spend in an average month. This is a really good exercise to do, and to repeat in detail once a year, because you may be slightly shocked at how the costs of those, apparently, insignificant coffees, lunches out, impulse purchases etc. start to add up.

Current Financial Position - Assets and Liabilities Summary Sheet

Assumed jointly owned – if not, please state

ASSETS		Current Value	LIABILITIES		Amount Outstanding
Main Residence			Main mortgage		
Other property			2nd mortgage		
Car(s)			Car Loan / Finance		
Savings	Bank		Other loans		
	Building Society				
	NS&I				
Investments	ISAs		Credit Cards		
	Unit Trusts				
	Investment Bonds				
	Other				
Other e.g.			Other e.g.		
	Company Shares			Income tax due	
	Art / fine wine			Mortgage arrears	
	Antiques			Personal debts	
	TOTAL ASSETS			TOTAL LIABILITIES	
				TOTAL NET WORTH	0

Figure 3. Assets and Liabilities Summary Sheet

Download the above spreadsheet at: www.dare2befair.com

This spreadsheet captures the value of your assets and the value of your debts or liabilities. Simplistically, this is summarising for you what you own, and what you owe.

A review of your assets can start with your cash savings: whether you have enough to cover your emergency funds and any big, planned expenditure in the next few years; if you have more than this, how to get it working harder for you by potentially investing it. Leaving too much cash sitting in the bank or in Premium Bonds only earning a very low level of interest means that your money is not keeping pace with inflation, which is the rising cost of goods.

Over time, inflation has a corrosive effect on the value of your savings and means that your money will not buy as much in the future as it does today. This is of particular concern for retirees, who often rely on their savings to provide additional spending money, alongside their pension income.

The Actual Effect of Inflation Over the Last 15 Years

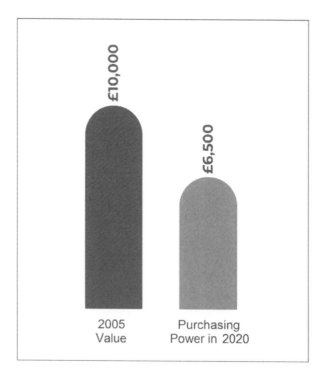

Figure 4. Effect of Inflation Over the Last 15 Years

Source: RPI All Items Index to January 2020, Office for National Statistics

Left to the effects of inflation, £10,000 in the bank over the last 15 years would have lost 35% of its purchasing power. Its purchasing value in 2020 would only be £6,500.

Our longer life expectancy means that protecting our money against the effects of inflation is hugely important. Otherwise, there is a very real risk that we will outlive the money we have.

Going back to the spreadsheet, summarising your debts will prompt you to review your mortgage, confirming how much is left to pay and how many years remain. Do you have life assurance in place which would repay the mortgage in the event of your death, enabling the surviving partner and family to remain living in the house should they wish to? Will your mortgage be paid off before you plan to retire? If not, will your pension income in retirement cover the mortgage repayments adequately?

It's also important to review any other debts or loans you have, and in particular, credit cards. If you are regularly using your overdraft every month or using credit cards and not fully repaying them every month, you could be incurring significant levels of interest.

Ideally, you should never be in a position where you are paying interest on a credit card, and if you are, then your number one priority is to pay it off in full, as quickly as possible.

The difference in value between your assets and your liabilities is known as your net worth. This can be important for the longer term when considering whether your estate will need to pay inheritance tax when you die.

The current rate of inheritance tax is an eye-watering 40%. There is an amount you can pass on *before* paying inheritance tax, known as the nil rate band and the residence nil rate band, and this value depends on your marital status and whether your estate includes a house that will pass directly to children or grandchildren. The tax-free amount currently ranges from £325,000 to £1 million depending on these factors.

There are caveats and small print to be aware of, but also many legitimate and HMRC-approved ways of structuring your estate to minimise the amount of inheritance tax your estate has to pay, which ensures that your beneficiaries get the maximum benefit possible from your assets on death.

Going back briefly to the spreadsheet, you may notice that there is nowhere to summarise pensions. This is because, whilst pensions are assets, they are considered to be outside of your estate for inheritance tax purposes. Therefore any lump sum death benefits or the remaining balance in the pension pot on death are not subject to inheritance tax. This is not to ignore pensions, far from it! They are likely to be your most valuable asset after your house, but they should be reviewed separately from your other assets.

If you are in a relationship, I recommend you complete this spreadsheet and discuss it with your partner. What is it showing you, and are there things that you want or need to change?

What is Investing?

Let's start with some of the basics. What is investing and why is it important?

The dictionary definition of investing is: to put money into financial schemes, shares, property or a commercial venture with the expectation of achieving a profit.

Put simply, investing is putting aside money now to have more money in future.

Putting aside money means money that you don't need to spend in the short term, i.e. the next four to five years, and that is put aside for the medium to longer term, ideally five to ten years or longer.

When I am advising clients, my definition of a healthy timeframe for an investment is a minimum of five years.

It's important because it can protect the value of your money from the effects of inflation, as we have just been looking at. But how does investing work?

The Eighth Wonder of the World

This is the perfect time to explain the wonder of compounding. Albert Einstein is reported to have called it "the most powerful force in the universe" and stated, "compound interest is the eighth wonder of the world."

When you save money in a bank account, you may earn some interest. Using a simple example, if you save £1,000 and earn interest of 2%, at the end of the first year you will have £1,020. The 2% interest is an additional £20 in your account.

At the end of the second year, a further 2% interest is added: 2% of the higher £1,020 is £20.40, so your total is now £1,040.40.

At the end of the 3rd year, 2% interest adds £20.81 so your total is £1,061.21.

Compounding is the effect of, not only your original capital earning interest, but the interest itself earning interest.

In the world of investing, we substitute the word interest for growth or returns, different words used to mean the same thing, making it potentially more confusing.

I should make it clear at this stage that investment returns do not occur in a straight line. The value of assets and therefore investments goes down as well as up, and you may get back less than you invested. Past performance does not guarantee future performance. You may be familiar with these disclaimers, and they should always be taken into consideration. I am simplifying everything to demonstrate the principle of investment returns, but please be mindful of the real-life variability that can occur each year.

£1,000 Investment Growing at 5% Per Year for 3 Years

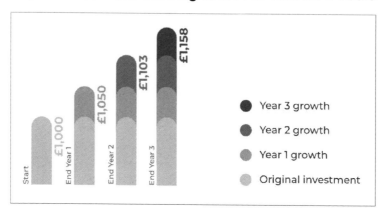

Figure 5. £1,000 Investment Growing at 5% Per Year for 3 Years

Imagine your £1,000 is invested and achieving growth of 5% per year.

At the end of Year 1, your £1,000 has become £1,050. At the end of Year 2, it is £1,103 and at the end of year 3, it is £1,158.

The higher the % growth or interest, the greater your return, added to the golden rule of investing, which is time.

The longer you leave your money invested, the greater the effect of compounding.

£1,000 Investment Growing at 5% Per Year for 20 Years

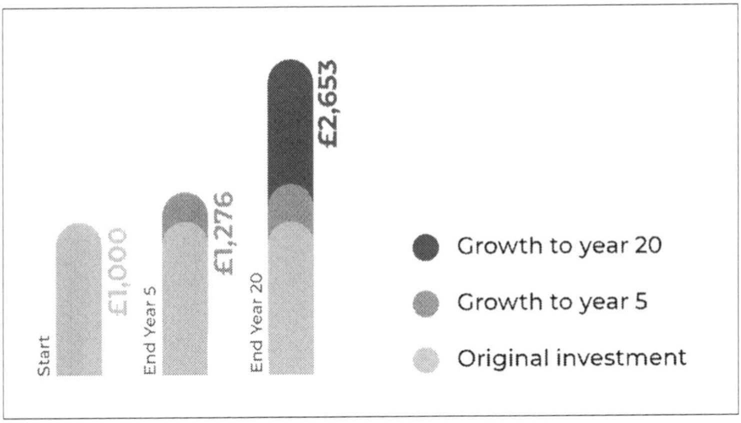

Figure 6. £1,000 Investment Growing at 5% Per Year for 20 Years

£1,000 invested for 5 years achieving 5% growth per year will be worth £1,276 — an extra £276. But if you leave it invested for 20 years at 5% growth per year, it becomes £2,653 — an extra £1,653.

This is why it's so important to be investing into a pension because it will remain invested for decades, through your working life. The more you invest when you are younger, the longer it has to grow. If you delay investing, because you are prioritising your short-term needs as discussed earlier, it is very costly to catch up in later life.

Let's look at an example from the other way round. Let's say you want to retire at age 60 with an annual income of £50,000.

To achieve this comfortably, without a fear of your money running out before you do, even if you live to 120, you ideally need a pension pot of £1 million.

Let's assume that any money you pay in grows at an average of 5% per year, after the effect of inflation of 2% a year. You should always take inflation into account when projecting values a long way into the future, due to the corrosive effect it can have on your spending power.

If you start paying in at age 20, you will need to fund £1,000 per month, combined across your and your employer's contributions, if you are employed. Again, I'm using a simple example, assuming that your monthly contributions never increase, even though the reality is, they will if your salary increases.

If you delay starting to pay in until you're 30, then to achieve the same pot of £1 million, over 30 years rather than 40 years, you'll need to pay in £1,700 per month. And if you delay starting pension contributions until you're 40, you'll need to pay in £3,000 per month for 20 years.

Monthly Pension Contributions Needed to Create a Pension Pot of £1 Million at Age 60

Figure 7. Monthly Pension Contributions Needed to Create a Pension Pot of £1 Million at Age 60

So, first lesson is to start as early as you can.

Second lesson is to pay in as much as you can afford, especially in the earlier years, as this can reduce how much you need to pay in later years.

I Love Stocks & Shares ISAs

A great way of investing for the long-term, which has the advantage of not only being very tax-efficient but also allowing you to take money out at any age, is to invest in an Individual Savings Account (ISA), specifically a Stocks & Shares ISA. The investment grows tax-free and the money you draw out is completely tax-free as well. No income tax or capital gains tax to pay.

The type of ISA you might be most familiar with is a cash ISA, offered by banks and building societies. They offer interest rates that are similar to their deposit and savings account rates, meaning they are currently very low. Gone are the days of cash ISAs providing annual interest of 5% or 6% like they did in the 1990s. However, of course, back then, higher interest rates also meant higher mortgage rates and higher inflation, which we conveniently forget.

Cash ISAs are effectively redundant now, as we all have a personal tax-free savings allowance of up to £1,000 per tax year, so any interest earned in your bank and savings accounts up to that amount is tax-free anyway.

The alternative to a cash ISA is a Stocks & Shares ISA, also known as an Equity ISA. Equity is another word for a stock, or share in a company (again, three words meaning pretty much the same thing!). The name of this ISA is misleading, however, because you don't have to invest purely in stocks or shares, you can invest in other types of assets that are lower risk, such as bonds, or commercial property for example. Anyway, what it really means is that it is 'invested' rather than 'deposited'. The implication of this is that it is subject to investment risk and charges, unlike your money in the bank.

Let me briefly explain what a stock or a share is. The word 'stock' is more commonly used in the US, and the word 'share' more commonly used in the UK. If you buy a stock or a share of a company, you become a shareholder, i.e. you own a share. It is a real, tangible asset and its value is determined by the success of the company itself and by market forces. When analysts and other investors feel confident and optimistic about the future growth and profitability of the company and/or the sector it trades in, the value of the stock rises; when they feel nervous or are concerned about potential issues with the company or the broader industry sector, the value of the share falls.

The value of quoted shares on a stock market can vary significantly and particularly over short time periods - a day, a week, a month, or a year.

When I advise clients on investing, I am working with a medium to long-term timeframe in mind, upwards of 5 years, and this is very different to day trading and speculating over short timeframes which are much higher risk activities. You are more likely to time it wrong, make the wrong judgement call and lose money.

If you want to speculate and try and earn a quick bang for your buck, there's nothing wrong with that, but that's not investing. It's certainly not sensible to be speculating with money that you need to fund your lifestyle in the future. It's fine for your beer / wine money, not for your pension fund.

Now whilst you can buy individual stocks and shares directly, this concentrates the risk into a small number of companies and doesn't create a diverse investment.

An alternative way is to invest in stocks and shares via collective funds. Here your money is pooled together with thousands of other investors, to buy shares in a wide range of companies. The fund is often managed by a professional investor, a fund manager. There are many different funds investing in different types of assets, not just stocks & shares. This allows you to spread your risk and invest in other types of assets and in a far broader range of companies than buying individual company shares yourself.

As the value of the funds grow, so your investment value grows. And here is another reality of successful investing: the longer the timeframe you invest, the greater your average annual returns are likely to be. The length of time you are invested for is a key driver of your final outcome and can be a more significant factor than trying to 'time the market' – meaning trying to buy or pay into an investment at the point when you think the value is lower. There has been a lot of analysis done around this, to demonstrate that if you try and time the market, you are likely to get it wrong.

I am a huge fan of Stocks & Shares ISAs, investing in collective funds. You can currently invest up to £20,000 per tax year per adult, and on behalf of children under 18, up to £9,000 per tax year. This could be a great activity for grandparents to get involved in.

I Love Pensions Too

What images spring to mind when you hear or read the word pension? For some reason, it seems to make younger people cringe, even recoil, and stick their heads in the sand immediately.

It's often something that you feel isn't important for at least another 10, 20 or 30 years, and in the meantime, you have more important and quite frankly enjoyable things to spend your money on.

But being an ostrich with your head in the sand is an uncomfortable place to be. Ask anyone who hasn't lifted their head out of the sand until they are in their 50s when it might be too late to make a meaningful difference or improvement to what lies ahead.

At the age of 50, if you want to retire at 60, you have only 120 paydays left to influence your future pension and the income you will have to live on. At the age of 30, you have 360 paydays left, a much better number to be working with.

So if you're in your 20s or 30s, one key message I need you to take from this book is the importance of paying into a pension and paying as much as you can afford into it at the youngest age possible.

> *Pay in as much as you can afford, at the youngest age possible*

Demystifying Pensions

So what is a pension? The dictionary definition is that the word describes the regular *income* that you receive when you are no longer working, paid by the government and/or by a financial organisation. In daily language, we tend to use the word pension to also mean the pot of money itself or the company scheme that we are a member of.

To receive an income when we are no longer working, we have to pay into a pension scheme whilst we *are* working to build up its value. The pension scheme uses the money we have paid into it, plus the value of investment growth which boosts the overall value compared to what we have paid in, to provide an income at the earliest age of 55 (soon to become 57 in legislation). In the case of the government-paid State pension, our National Insurance contributions are used as payment into our future pension.

Investment growth within a pension is tax-free, the same as within an ISA, which maximises the potential return to you. Nowadays there are different ways in which a scheme provides an income and this is where it can start to feel complicated. But in all cases, up to 25% of the value of the pot can be taken tax-free, and the rest is taxable. It is taxed according to income tax rules, so the rate of tax you pay is determined by how much income you drawdown (receive) each tax year.

I don't intend to explain the different types of pension schemes here, just to mention them.

There are 2 main types: the older traditional schemes are known as *Defined Benefit schemes* (also called Final Salary schemes, now adjusted to be career average salary schemes) which still operate in the Public Sector. The more common workplace schemes in the Private Sector, which are personal pensions, are known as *Money Purchase schemes*. These are also referred to as Defined Contribution schemes, Group Personal Pensions, self-invested personal pensions (SIPPs), personal or private pensions. So much jargon!

How each type of scheme provides tax-free cash and taxable income varies, which is why it's so important to get information (from PensionWise.co.uk) or better still, financial advice tailored to your personal circumstances.

Choosing the right format of income for your circumstances at the time is critical because once you have made a decision, it cannot always be changed.

So your pension income is your salary when you stop working, and that's the most user-friendly way to think about it.

At the end of the day, despite the jargon and complexity, there are essentially only two types of pension: a big one or a small one! The bigger the pension, the more choices you have and the more income you will have — so size matters, and the bigger the better.

The reason the State wants to encourage people to build up their own pension provision is so they are less reliant on State Benefits in their retirement. To encourage regular pension savings, there are incentives known as tax reliefs, which add free money into your pension at the point you pay in.

If you are a non or basic rate taxpayer i.e. income less than £50,000 per tax year, based on today's thresholds, for every £80 you pay into a pension, HMRC adds £20. If you are a higher rate taxpayer with total income up to £150,000 per tax year, for every £60 you pay in, the government adds £40 via a combination of £20 direct contribution and £20 claimed back via self-assessment. And for additional rate taxpayers, for every £55 you pay in, you get £45 tax relief.

There are essentially only two types of pension: a big one or a small one. Size matters!

A word about the auto-enrolment policy that was introduced in October 2012 and represents a first step for employed workers to easily build a personal pension, in addition to the State Pension.

I say a first step as there are flaws, one of which is indirectly discriminatory against women. You have to earn a minimum of £192 per week or £10,000 per year to be automatically enrolled, but this has to be with just one employer. If you have 2 or 3 part-time jobs, which more women than men are likely to have, it doesn't matter if your total income is more than £10,000, you cannot access an auto-enrolment pension scheme which means you do not benefit from receiving contributions from your employer.

It is voluntary, not mandatory, and you can opt out within the first 28 days of being enrolled. You have to be above the age of 22, and it is not available to the self-employed, who need to set up their own pensions.

Not Working? No Problem

Even if you are not earning at all, you can still pay into a pension and receive tax relief. Many people don't know this. You can pay in up to £2,880 per tax year, which after 20% has been added, is £3,600 in total per year. So there is a mechanism for women who are not working, whether temporarily via a career break or permanently, to build their pension provision. See Chapter 4 for my specific recommendation on how working partners can, and should, continue to contribute into a pension for the benefit of their non-working wives.

This same mechanism enables parents and grandparents to invest on behalf of their children/grandchildren into a pension. Yes, children can have pension investments too.

The key thing to be aware of is that there is an age restriction on when you can start to take the money out of the pension. In the next decade, this minimum age will rise from 55 to 57 and is likely to increase further, the intention being to keep a 10-year gap between State Pension age and private pension access.

For contributing parents or grandparents, this can also provide personal tax planning benefits relative to inheritance tax. If these gifts are made from your surplus income, as opposed to cash savings, there is no 7-year rule and the value of the gift is outside your estate immediately for inheritance tax purposes.

Anyway, the point I want to illustrate is this: if you invest £5 a day for a child from birth to the age of 10, and then *stop paying in*, the pension investment could be worth £1 million when they are age 65, if the investment grows at an average of 7% per year.

£1 million for the cost of £150 per month for 10 years — what an amazing legacy to leave your children or grandchildren.

Emotions Play Their Part

The cycle of emotional investing that creates exhilaration when values are rising and despair when values are falling is well recognised in behavioural science. This is something your financial adviser can help you resist. They should stop you from making the wrong decisions as well as helping you make the right decisions.

Far too often, people who invest for themselves, without taking financial advice, will follow the herd. They will buy into trends that risk becoming a bubble, like Bitcoin has done in the past, and will take their money out when values crash because they are scared they will lose everything. They will then wait for values to recover and grow before putting their money back into the market. This is exactly the wrong way round if you are trying to achieve the most successful outcome.

Many personal financial decisions are made from a place of emotion, rather than from a spreadsheet. This comes back to my earlier point about the importance of having a goal, or an intention that sits behind any investment that you make. It may be tempting in future to move away from making those regular investments, to pay for a weekend break or something else that has cropped up unexpectedly.

However, if you have committed emotionally to building a nest egg for your children's future, or to having the holiday of a lifetime in five years to celebrate a milestone birthday, then you are far more likely to want to continue with that regular investment, even if it requires you to make some sacrifices in the short term.

If you are in a relationship, it's important to have those conversations together, to make sure that you both align and agree on your priorities and goals for the future. Then you can make a joint commitment to supporting and achieving those goals together.

Living the Dream

Planning for a great life in retirement is probably *the* most important goal for any individual or couple in their lifetime.

If you stop and think how devastating it would be, having worked so hard for decades to give yourself a good life, to get to the point when you finally stop working and realise that you don't have enough money to live on.

How upsetting would it be, knowing that there were times when you *did* have money that you could have put aside during those years, but because you didn't realise how important it was to balance your longer-term needs with your immediate priorities, you frittered that money away? "Frittered," isn't my word. It's a word that many of my clients in their 50s and 60s have used when they look back, regretfully, on what they could have done differently, if only they had realised...

The words retirement and pension may sound alien, and as humans, it doesn't always come naturally to plan for our future. It's like being told that if you keep smoking, when you're older you might die of lung cancer or some other equally horrible disease. Knowing it doesn't necessarily make us change our behaviour.

So my suggestion is to call that future stage of your life something more uplifting, something to look forward to. Think about what you'd like to be doing when you no longer have to work. It could be such a liberating time if you have enough money to do what you want to do.

It's potentially a time of your life when you will be free from many of the responsibilities that you may currently have on your plate: no longer paying a mortgage, no longer paying for your children's clothes, food, drink, school fees, petrol, car insurance etc. No longer responsible for employing people in your business, or managing people in your team. Maybe no longer caring for older relatives who have now passed on.

It is the one time in your life, ladies, where you may finally have the opportunity to focus on yourself for a change. And what we need are three things: enough time, enough money and enough good health.

If you don't have enough money, your time will no longer be your own as you are likely to still be working until you are 70 plus, which may well impact the state of your health. Money does indeed make the world go round.

So, why not call retirement something different, and re-name your retirement plan?

- It could be my "travel the world" plan.
- My "do whatever I want to do" plan.
- My "enjoy being a grandmother" plan.
- My "work in the local community" plan.
- My "move to a country cottage" plan.
- My "live at the beach" plan.

My husband's retirement plan is his "follow the England cricket team around the world" plan and my add-on is my "lie on a beautiful beach whilst my husband watches cricket" plan.

Use whatever is uppermost in your mind as your vision for how you want your life to look in retirement. This will focus your mind on exactly what it is you're trying to achieve and make it more enjoyable and motivating to invest towards it each month.

Making a Start

So, what are your next steps?

I encourage you to read more about what investing is and how to approach it. You can learn about different asset classes, the importance of diversifying and then consider how to use your tax allowances and exemptions effectively each year.

You can choose to work with a Financial Planner to help guide and advise you on what will be right for your circumstances and objectives. You have to pay for the advice, but this should result in better financial outcomes for you.

Use the materials in this chapter to assess your current situation, and to gain a sense of control and understanding. Identify your key goals for the future, and if in a relationship, discuss and agree on these with your partner.

Then you can decide if you are ready to step into the world of investing to build yourself a better financial future.

Establishing a financial plan and getting yourself involved in your financial situation will give you not only a sense of understanding but a sense of control too.

This, in turn, creates well-being. The more we understand and feel confident in what we are doing, and the reasons why, the more contented and secure we feel.

Having a clear financial plan can take away a lot of the worry and concern, and the potential feeling of being left out of important decisions within a relationship.

One lady I recently worked with explained that she had been worrying for years about whether she and her husband could afford to stay in their family home once they retired, even to the point of losing sleep about it. Encouraged by friends to confront her worry and get advice, I was delighted to tell her, having reviewed their situation, that they would be fine. If they invested to get some of their cash savings working harder for them, this combined with their pensions would give them enough income to enjoy their retirement in their family home, which was her number one priority.

I encourage you to do the same. Take the initiative and take control of your financial future.

Women make great financial decision-makers, and the level of knowledge you need to have to achieve this is not huge. Remember, no rule or truth says just because a man is earning a good salary, he is better with money than you are. In my experience, even men who work as financial directors or in financial services don't necessarily understand pensions, investing and tax planning any more than anyone else.

Creating a plan that gives you a good line of sight of what your future net worth and income could look like can inform and drive your decisions about your career and future earnings.

When you can see the effect your *own* financial contributions will have on your future life, it's likely to raise the level of importance in your mind of earning a fair and decent salary.

It might make you more determined to ask for that pay rise, or negotiate a higher bonus, because you can attach a tangible significance to it, both in the here and now and the future.

It might also make you think differently about giving it up when you start a family.

Exercise:

I've created a checklist to help you evaluate how financially in control you are:

Be fully conscious of your own situation and consider, as you read the rest of the book – whether you are happy with it or whether you want to change it.

1. Do I know my current bank balance?

2. Do I know exactly what I spend each month?

3. Do I understand what an ISA is?

4. Do I know the difference between a cash ISA, a Lifetime ISA and a Stocks & Shares ISA?

5. What level of cash saving do I have?

6. Is this enough to act as emergency funds, i.e. is it about 3 months' worth of expenditure?

7. Am I putting money aside via savings or investments for a particular reason or goal?

8. Do I know how much I owe on the mortgage, and how many years are remaining on the loan?

9. If I use credit cards, do I know what interest rate is being charged?

10. Do I know how many weeks of sick pay my employer would pay me for?

11. If I'm self-employed, do I have or need Income Protection, to provide a replacement salary if I am incapacitated and cannot work for a while?

12. Do I have life assurance in place to pay off my mortgage and provide funds for my family to live on, if I died?

13. Have I thought about what age I want to start a family?

14. For existing children, am I saving on their behalf? Do I want them to own money and have control of it at 18 or younger? Or do I want them to be older before they can spend it?

15. Do I want to pay for private school fees and at what age or stage of education?

16. Have I ever thought about what age I want to stop working, and how? Gradual transition into retirement or a hard stop?

17. Do I know what my pensions will be worth when I retire? Do I know how much income they will give me and whether that will be enough?

18. Have I updated my old pension providers every time I've moved house or changed my name, so they can keep in contact with me?

19. How much of this list have I discussed with my partner?

20. Do I know what is in his or her mind for these important questions?

Download this checklist at: www.dare2befair.com

CHAPTER 4

Taking Control Before a Crisis

"I am prepared for the worst, but hope for the best."

- Benjamin Disraeli

> *In this chapter you will learn:*
>
> - important financial considerations for divorce
> - how to manage bereavement
> - how to safeguard financially against ill health or early death

Fix the Roof Whilst the Sun is Shining

With most things in life, having a plan means that you are better prepared if a crisis or unexpected tragedy occurs. Your finances are the same.

Being as prepared as possible, should the unexpected happen, is a good financial planning goal. The Covid-19 pandemic has perhaps shown us this, better than anything in recent history.

It seems to be a human trait that we all consider ourselves to be invincible, particularly from the risk of serious illness or worse. Yet, if I ask you if you know anyone who has been diagnosed with a serious illness, which has meant that they've been unable to work for quite a few months, or anyone who's died young, then the chances are you can probably name someone.

And yet we never think it will happen to us.

As well as the risk of early death or ill health, we should also prepare for the possibility of the end of a long-term relationship or divorce.

You may believe that the divorce process will sort out your finances fairly, should it come to that. However, I have to tell you that this is often far from reality.

There is usually so much emotion involved in agreeing on a financial settlement as part of a divorce, and each side is reliant on the other to provide full disclosure of all assets held in their name. Sometimes this doesn't happen, and if you don't know what assets are in your name and what are in your partner's name — particularly if there are business assets involved — then you are unlikely to know for sure whether everything is being disclosed as it should be.

It's far better to have a good understanding of your financial situation and who owns what, well before finding yourself in this difficult situation.

Agreeing on a Fair Divorce Settlement

So what happens if your relationship breaks down? What happens if you are no longer going to be sharing your future with the person you thought you would still be married to or living with? Your financial security can suddenly be turned upside down.

I'm going to look at divorce very deliberately from the stereotypical perspective where the man is earning more than the woman, and the woman has reduced her earnings or stopped work completely to raise children.

Having been through a divorce myself in my early 30s, I have my own experience to draw on. However, you soon appreciate that everyone's experience of it is different and unique. Even when the breakup is amicable, the whole process of formal divorce can still be difficult, emotional and prolonged.

At the other extreme, if there are unresolved emotional issues such as anger, bitterness, jealousy, extreme hurt, agreeing on a financial settlement that both parties feel is fair and are happy with can be nigh on an impossible task.

You may find yourself having to respond and negotiate your financial future at a time of real crisis, rather than having time and mental space to think things through clearly.

Often when facing divorce, a woman's instinct for self-preservation and protecting her children means that her priorities are very short term. The immediate needs and considerations are many and varied. Will I have enough money to live on? Will I be able to remain in the house? If there are children involved, what will the financial support be? What will the access rights be?

Trying to resolve all of these aspects and coming to an agreement you find fair and acceptable is likely to take up a lot of time and energy. There will be many things, big and small, to consider, negotiate and ultimately compromise on.

Emotion may override financial objectivity and this is why working with a good Family Law solicitor, rather than personally trying to reach an agreement, is likely to give you a better financial outcome. Even though there is a cost involved, it may be the best decision you make, in terms of securing a better long-term financial future for yourself.

My plea to you is to appreciate how critical it is to agree on your long-term position as well as the short term. This financial settlement cannot normally be revised in the future. The divorce is your only opportunity to ensure that you agree on a settlement that will recognise fairly the contributions you have made to the relationship throughout the years you have been together, and which will stand you in good stead for your future life.

I'm specifically referring to the huge importance of pensions within the financial settlement. After the house, the pensions, *his* pensions, are likely to be the next highest value asset.

However, as we've touched on before, pensions are difficult and complex to understand, and so many women shy away from them. They may avoid discussing pensions with their ex because they feel they don't have the knowledge or understanding of what they are and how they work. Therefore, what often transpires is that the importance of pensions is undervalued in the discussion about asset sharing.

I've worked with several women post-divorce who have said "it was so traumatic just to get to the point of agreeing on the immediate maintenance support and whether we could remain in the house, I just couldn't bear another argument and another confrontation about the pensions, so I let it go."

I feel desperately sad and angry when I hear those words. I don't see why it should be an either/or situation of negotiation between the short term and the longer term; especially if there are children from the marriage and the woman has given up her career to be at home with them, thus sacrificing her earnings potential for the good of the family.

Not working, or scaling back her career, will have affected the woman in several critical ways:

1. She is unlikely to have been paying into a personal pension to build provision for the future, and will not have been receiving contributions from an employer.

2. The longer she remains outside the workforce, the greater the impact on her earnings potential if she returns to work in future.

3. If the children are still of school age, it may be unlikely that she can return to work *full-time* after the divorce, whether she is currently working part-time or not at all.

Most solicitors will be advising their clients to take pension assets into account although, currently, it is not mandatory. Several organisations are specifically campaigning for pension-sharing to be a mandatory consideration, if not outcome, in all divorces, which I support 100%.

As solicitors are not trained in pension technicalities in the way Financial Planners are, it's often a good idea for them to work together on this, for the benefit of the divorcee.

If the pensions are undervalued and not fully understood, it is likely that the woman will walk away from the relationship with a significant financial disadvantage. It's not enough to just take into account the *current* value of the pensions; their value needs to be understood at the age of retirement, with consideration being given as to how much each side will be contributing between now and then.

This could be many years into the future, and inequalities of pension value and contribution amounts will make the two outcomes diverge. If the man is going to be working full time, he will be making ongoing pension contributions as well as his employer doing so, often rising in value as his salary rises. So the actual value of his pension pot when he comes to retire may be vastly higher than its current value.

This must therefore be taken into account when considering what percentage split is appropriate *now*. If the woman is unlikely to ever be earning at a similar level to the man over the next 10, 20, 30 years, she will not be accumulating the same level of pension provision and this should be compensated for by granting the woman a higher share of the pension now, rather than a default 50/50 split. This can provide a strong rationale for the solicitor to use in discussions and negotiations with the other side.

When both sides are trying to agree on things themselves rather than working through solicitors, it is much more difficult to ensure this is achieved. Emotions can get in the way, and if one side is financially stronger and more literate, it's easy to see how the imbalance of financial knowledge and confidence can produce an unfair outcome, usually, but not always, for the woman.

Life After Bereavement

The second crisis subject I want to talk about is bereavement.

This can potentially happen at any stage of life, although of course, it's more likely to happen when we are older. There is generally a significant difference in the generations around financial understanding and preparedness.

If a woman in her 70s or older is widowed, she has grown up in an era when women did not get as involved in the finances. She is likely to be in the difficult situation of not knowing much about her current financial situation, in terms of what assets are where, and also feeling daunted and overwhelmed about having to manage it all herself going forwards. I know my mum and many in her generation acknowledge that they would feel lost, not knowing how to start managing their finances.

I should say that this can also be a challenge for many women who are going through a divorce. The thought of having to take control of their finances in the future can be scary enough to lead them to stay in the relationship for longer than they want to, in order not to face this challenge. I have personal experience of this amongst my friends.

This feels like a soul-destroying reason to stay in a relationship with somebody that you don't want to be with, especially when there is help and support out there in the shape of good financial planners to help you make the right decisions.

When it comes to bereavement, the emotions and mindset can be quite different to facing a divorce, but in both situations there is usually the process of grieving to go through.

Shock can also be a factor in both situations if the death or separation is very sudden and unexpected. This is where not being prepared, not knowing what assets you have, where they are and whose name they are in, can be a complicating factor.

This is particularly true also for debts. Sometimes it's not only until these points of crisis that the true financial picture emerges. Unfortunately, sometimes there are debts that you knew nothing about. And worse still, you can sometimes be jointly liable for them even if you are not the one who has accumulated them.

This was dramatised in the TV series Finding Alice in which the husband died suddenly from an accidental fall, and the wife was oblivious to the fact that the husband had real issues with his business, and they were in a lot of debt.

This awful revelation can fundamentally change the way you view the person who's died, if you realise that they were not being completely honest with you about your financial situation, or if in fact, they had been deceiving you.

This is fortunately not the experience for most people, but it's worth asking yourself "how much do I really know?" It all points to the same reality, which is, the more involved you are with your partner in both your personal and business finances, the more likely you are to know what's going on.

Let's return to the older generation and the consequences of bereavement from a financial point of view. Given that women still tend to live longer than men, it is quite probable that a widowed woman is faced not only with the emotions of having to deal with the loss of her life partner but also facing a significant financial hit in terms of pension income.

The relevant issue here is that if the man was receiving a pension income from a Final Salary scheme (which most people over the age of 60 do) there is a significant reduction to that income once he dies. The widow will typically receive only 50% of the income, or at best 66%.

Final salary schemes, which were the main type of pension set up by employers until 1988, when personal pensions were first introduced, were designed to reward loyalty and longevity of service of the employees, therefore usually disproportionately benefitting the men.

On death, through no fault of her own or her husband, the wife's income can be halved. What a way to compensate women who have not worked in order to raise children! The same is often true if the pension income is being paid by an annuity. If any widow's pension has been factored in at all, it's likely to be a much lower % than the man was receiving, and often there is no widow's pension.

I should point out that in some cases, if you are not married at the time of death, as a widow you may not be eligible for any ongoing pension. It will depend on the scheme's rules and whether your financial dependence can be taken into account, rather than just your marital status.

This can have dire consequences on whether the widow can afford to maintain her standard of living. It can lead to having to move out of her home to downsize.

Fortunately, this is one area that is changing and is likely to continue changing positively for future generations of women. Most private sector companies are no longer offering Final Salary pensions, but Money Purchase pensions instead. On death, the *full value* of the Money Purchase or Drawdown pension pot is available to the widow. Additionally, there is no requirement to be married to be a beneficiary.

The upshot of this, for future generations, is that a widow may still have access to the same level of income as she had when her partner was alive, as long as there is enough money in the pension pot to support her for the rest of her life.

Pension regulation is evolving to better suit our modern lives but I believe it can go further. There is now the option to convert a Final Salary pension into a Money Purchase or Drawdown pension in certain circumstances. If this can be more widely implemented, it has the power to benefit women significantly.

The regulator, the Financial Conduct Authority (FCA), rightly has concerns over whether this course of action is suitable for some people's circumstances, and anyone considering this is required to take financial advice.

It would be good, in my view, for the FCA to fully recognise the significance of this option for women specifically, and the effect it can have on their financial resources once widowed. I would like to see it soften its default position that Final Salary pensions are best retained and not converted. As explained it can potentially make the difference between a widowed woman having just half the pension income to live on, or the same amount as when her husband or partner was alive.

After a bereavement is a key time to receive good financial advice. However, it's not a good idea to make any big decisions immediately. It's always important to have a friend or family member present in any meetings to ensure that the right decisions are being made at the right time and that decisions are not being made on the spur of the moment or under any sort of duress.

Protect Against the Unexpected

The third financial crisis is suffering ill-health or having an accident which means you can't work for a period of time.

If you are self-employed, your ability to earn an income may stop immediately, and then how will you keep paying the bills?

If you are employed, you will receive a certain level of sick pay for the time that you are incapacitated and off work. Firstly, do you know how many weeks' sick pay your employer will pay you? It will be stated in your contract. And what happens after that point if you're not well enough to return to work? Some of you will have generous employee benefits which include income protection — a replacement salary provided by an insurance policy that your employer pays for. This policy will start paying out after the employer's period of sick pay has finished. The money is tax-free and therefore often fully replaces the gross income you would have earned whilst working.

Other employees may not have such generous benefits. Once the employer's sick pay period has ended, which could be just a few weeks, the only pay you would receive is Statutory Sick Pay (SSP) for up to 28 weeks. In the 2021/22 tax year, SSP is £96.35 per week and there are certain eligibility criteria you have to meet to receive it.

This is unlikely to pay the bills, so if you are in this situation, or if you are self-employed and have no employee benefits, you should consider taking out an Income Protection policy to provide a replacement salary.

There are various features you can build into the policy, to tailor it to your situation, for example, how quickly it starts paying out. The more weeks that pass before it starts, the cheaper the monthly premiums, which is where having a good level of cash savings as an emergency fund is important.

You might be reading this thinking "well I'm healthy, I never take time off work." But what if you're diagnosed with cancer and have to undergo treatment? What if you have a stroke or a heart attack and need time to recover? What if you break your back and have to lie flat for months while you heal?

Wouldn't it be great to have peace of mind, knowing that if something like this did happen to you or your partner, you wouldn't have to rush back to work because you needed to start earning again? You could take the time you need to fully recover, with the insurance policy paying the bills for you. The peace of mind this type of policy provides can be invaluable.

You may also have heard of a different type of policy called Critical Illness cover, which pays out a lump sum rather than a monthly income. It is often taken out when you start a mortgage and apply for life assurance which repays the mortgage in the event of death.

For most people, making the monthly mortgage repayment is the single biggest expense on their spreadsheet. Therefore if a lump sum is available to repay some or all of that mortgage at a time when you are seriously ill, it provides the same peace of mind and can take the pressure off.

The situations in which it pays out are more restricted than with Income Protection. As the name suggests, you have to be diagnosed with a specific Critical Illness for the policy to pay out. Over 85% of claims paid out are due to heart attack, stroke, cancer and multiple sclerosis — the 'big four' — but the policies typically cover a broad range of serious health conditions. However it doesn't pay out for other reasons such as having an accident, so you need to consider what's right for your personal situation.

The final type of protection to mention is a life insurance policy, which pays out in the event of you dying.

This is therefore very relevant to the subject of bereavement. If you have a mortgage, especially a joint mortgage, it's very important you have this type of policy in place. If one of you dies during the term of the mortgage, and the surviving partner is not able to afford the mortgage repayments based on their income, the lender can insist the property is sold so that the loan can be repaid immediately.

Imagine the nightmare scenario of a sudden bereavement at a stage of life when you still have a mortgage. The last thing you would want, whilst coming to terms with the shock and grief, is facing the possibility of having to sell the house and finding somewhere else to live.

Life Assurance is relatively cheap, because the risk of dying young is low, so it should be affordable. An early death may also mean that you have children who are still financially dependent on you and this type of policy can also provide funds for the family to live on. This is particularly important if it's the main breadwinner who dies.

Employees in larger companies may have a Death in Service (DIS) benefit which would pay out to the family, but it's still a good idea to have a separate policy to repay the mortgage. Your DIS is only available to you whilst you are employed by that company. If you change jobs in future and find that you don't have a similar benefit, it will be more expensive for you if you're older to set up a separate life assurance policy.

One thing to highlight, in the interests of fairness to women, is that it's better to have a life assurance policy each if you have a joint mortgage, rather than taking out a joint policy. Having a policy in your sole name means that, should you end up divorcing or separating, you can choose whether to continue with the policy or cancel it. If it's a joint policy and your ex wants to cancel it, they can. Having two separate policies, therefore, means that you can make the decision yourself and retain control of your situation.

Be Aware and Be Prepared

So in summary, we can never know what's around the corner.

We don't know if bereavement, ill health or divorce may come upon us. Being aware and involved in your finances is the best way of being prepared should such an event happen. It gives you the best chance to come out the other side positively, without financial worries and with a clear understanding of your financial future.

Having adequate protection in place is a key part of any good financial plan, to give security and peace of mind to you as a family when you need to protect your home and your children. It puts you in a much stronger financial position if a crisis hits.

Key Actions From This Chapter:

- Talk openly with your partner about your assets and liabilities: what you own and what you owe. Make sure you both know about each other's assets including pensions. Be honest about any issues such as overdue credit cards or business loans.

- If your partner is the main breadwinner and handles the money, ask him to talk you through what the situation would be if he were to die.

- If you're employed, check out all of your Employee Benefits: how long is your sick pay period, is it extended with an Income Protection policy, do you have a Death in Service benefit?

- If you're self-employed and your earnings would stop or reduce if you were unable to work, put in place Income Protection.

- Make sure you have cash savings for emergency funds.

- Review any existing life assurance policies you have and check if they still match your mortgage. Does the sum you are insured for cover your current mortgage, and is the policy valid until the year the mortgage ends? Often when we change our mortgage, maybe borrow more or extend the number of years, we don't change our life assurance policy leaving ourselves under-insured. If you're going to pay for insurance, it should be fit for purpose and covering all that you need it to.

- If you run your own company, do you have Key Person Insurance in place to protect the company's revenue or profit in the event of a key person within the business dying or being off sick?

CHAPTER 5

The Big Decision – Career Versus Children

"Life isn't about finding yourself. Life is about creating yourself."

– George Bernard Shaw

In this chapter you will learn:

- the long-term financial consequences of taking a career break or working part-time
- conversations to have with your partner as well as your employer
- how to financially compensate yourself if you're not working full-time

---

Your Biggest Financial Decision

I've been deliberately provocative with the title of this chapter. I don't mean to imply that career and children are really on opposite sides of the same decision. Of course, it's perfectly possible to combine the two, and many women do so very successfully.

It's a question of degree and trying to find a balance that works for you, your partner and your child or children. Some women make a clear decision one way or the other, whether to give up their career, particularly whilst their children are young if it's financially viable for the family.

The purpose of this chapter is not to judge in any way. It is to highlight what a huge financial decision this can be for you and how it will affect your longer-term financial security, which you may be completely unaware of. I explore the impacts from a career, earnings and financial perspective, as well as touching on the potential effects on self-esteem.

The decision whether to return to work after having a baby or what hours to work, should not just be about immediate affordability, or just about whether you can live as a family on one person's income, normally the higher earner.

The other driving force is your view and preference on how to support and raise your children and whether you want to be at home with them full-time. This chapter will give you another equally important aspect to consider: the long-term financial consequences of the decisions that you make at this time.

I have chosen to dedicate a whole chapter to this because I think it's the single most important decision that affects career progression, earnings, the gender pay gap and the gender pensions gap.

Can We Have it All?

I realise it is not a simple binary choice between career and children. For the vast majority of women, the two are combined, partly through positive choice and often through financial necessity.

Those of us who grew up in the 1980s were told we could "have it all" and I'm a classic example of someone who has strived to do just that. We were encouraged to believe we could be superwoman, pursuing our full-time career whilst being the perfect mum and that we would love it. It's not as easy as all that.

In my experience, there is no such thing as giving equal priority to your career and your children. Ultimately one has to be prioritised over the other during certain periods of your life, at least in terms of the time you spend on each. Striking an equal 50/50 balance is almost impossible to achieve.

When I had my son in 1997, women generally either returned to work full-time or left the company. There was no part-time option for roles that were considered business-critical.

Whilst the company I worked for had a collaborative and supportive culture, if you scratched under the surface or started to challenge the norm, they weren't able to cope or accommodate it. A friend of mine, who had re-joined the workforce full-time after her maternity leave, asked to reduce her hours to 4 days a week after a few months and was given a swift "no." She had even prepared a proposal of how her current job could be altered to accommodate this reduction in hours, and how the work she was currently doing could be picked up in other parts of the business. She took a couple of days to think about it and then resigned.

It felt to me like a travesty that she had to make that decision. So stark, without any attempt by the company to fully consider the proposal, and they lost a great employee as a result.

Fortunately, it wasn't long after that that the law changed and employers are now required to consider requests for part-time work. If the answer is no, then a clear rationale has to be provided to explain why not.

Part-time working after maternity leave was then hailed as a break-through and the perfect solution for working mums in the late 1990s and through the 2000s. And the uptake was high.

However, I believe it may have become a double-edged sword and is now holding women back from having greater success and fulfil-ment in their careers.

Society now seems to expect mums with babies and children to work part-time rather than full-time. It's been a subtle development, almost as if, now the choice exists to work part-time, why wouldn't you?

I'm about to explain one very good reason why you might *not* want to work part-time. I will highlight the negative consequences that working part-time has on a woman's financial situation, and also how this can impact self-esteem and confidence.

When you go from a situation in which you have been fully contrib-uting to the household finances, pre-children, and this changes due to a career break or part-time working, it can have a debilitating effect on your sense of worth.

Yes, you've become a mum which is a wonderful thing and can boost your self-confidence in fulfilling this most female of roles, but it can come at the expense of your previous identity and your role as a financial contributor to the family. The effect may not be immediate, although it is for some women, but it can certainly build over time.

It can become a vicious circle, particularly when weighing up the financial pros and cons of returning to work part-time. You start to think "what I could earn now is not as important as it used to be, and it's not as important as my partner's income. He earns more and we can live on his earnings alone. So there's no need for me to work."

This way of thinking can undermine your feelings of self-worth and confidence. It is a limiting belief that your unconscious mind repeats until it becomes your reality. "My money's not important."

Should you ever want or need to return to the workplace, you are more likely to accept a lower-paid role or a lower grade role because you no longer have the confidence to go back into the role you were perfectly capable of doing before you had children; even though you have developed new valuable skills whilst being on maternity leave, in addition to what you had before.

There are a whole series of negative consequences that can result from this reduced financial role for women within the family.

Seeing the Full Picture

I now want to spell out the financial implications of working part-time or taking a career break.

I have three case studies of women aged 30, all earning £30,000 a year before having their first child:

1. Emma decides to return to work full time after her maternity leave.

2. Alesha decides to take an extended break from the work-place for 2 years before returning to work.

3. Louise decides to return to work part-time, working 3 days a week and continue this for the next 10 years before returning to full-time work, once her child is older.

For all three, I consider their salary and pension contributions over the next 30 years and show what difference their work choices have on their financial situation in the future.

To keep things straightforward, I assume that in all cases, each woman has 8% of her salary paid in as pension contributions (which is the auto-enrolment minimum, and which, by the way, is usually not enough to give you the income you need in retirement). That each woman's employer applies an annual pay rise of 1.5%. That for Emma and Louise, their maternity leave is for 6 months, during which time they continue to receive 100% of their salary and pension contributions.

I assume their pension investment grows at 5% per annum.

The absolute numbers are not important, it is the comparison between the numbers that tells the story.

Base Case Salary Comparisons

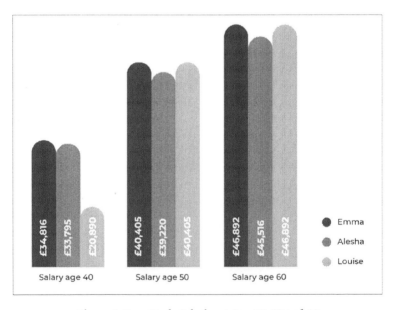

Figure 8. Case Study Salaries at Age 40, 50 and 60

What conclusions can we draw from this?

Firstly, apart from the obvious difference in salary for Louise in the years she is working part-time, rather than full-time, the differences in salary over time may not seem that great. However, remember that these salaries are being paid every year, so a small difference each year adds up to a lot more over time.

Alesha's 2 years out of the workplace reduces her salary by 3% compared to Emma's, which is never regained.

Apart from 6 months of fully paid maternity leave, Emma's time in the workplace is much more typical of a man's working life, in that it is continuous.

If Louise has a smooth transition from 3 days a week back to full-time at age 40, without any salary reduction, then the impact of her part-time work is confined to those 10 years, and she is then back on track with Emma.

But look at the effect these different decisions have on their pensions.

Base Case Pension Pot Comparisons

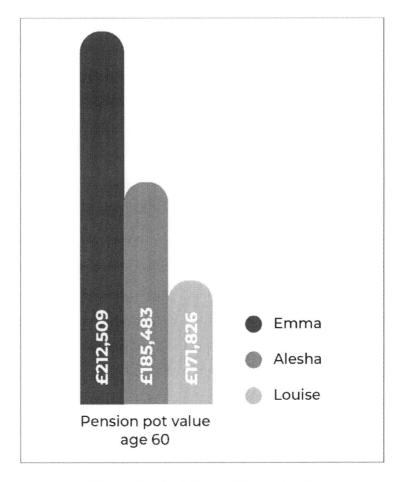

Figure 9. Case Study Pension Values at Age 60

At the age of 60, the effect of Louise working part-time for 10 years reduces her pension pot by *nearly 20%* compared to Emma.

The difference in the value of contributions going into her pension is 12% but the effect of compounding over 30 years makes the outcome for Louise much worse, increasing the final difference to 20%.

For Alesha, the effect of not working for just 2 years, reduces her pension contributions by 8% compared to Emma, and the final effect on her pension pot is that it's worth 13% less at the age of 60.

This degree of difference has a substantial impact on the amount of pension income you have to live on in retirement.

Real Life

Some of the assumptions I've made here do not take account of what is highly likely to happen in real life. Let's overlay some assumptions about how these women may be treated differently when they return to work in terms of career progression and salary:

1. Emma, who has barely missed a beat since giving birth, is promoted at the age of 32, receiving a 10% salary increase, and is promoted again 5 years later, with a further 10% salary increase (as well as the annual inflationary rises of 1.5%).

2. When Alesha returns to work after a 2-year career break, she finds she is not able to achieve the same job grade and salary she was on before and accepts a lower grade job with a 10% lower salary.

3. When Louise completes 10 years of part-time work and wants to revert to full-time, she is unable to find a role that matches her full-time equivalent salary and accepts a full-time role with a 20% lower salary.

I hope you agree that these assumptions are by no means crazy, and in fact, they are very realistic. I don't need to exaggerate the assumptions to demonstrate what significant differences these real-life scenarios have on each of the women. Particularly on their pension pot values.

Real Life Salary Comparisons

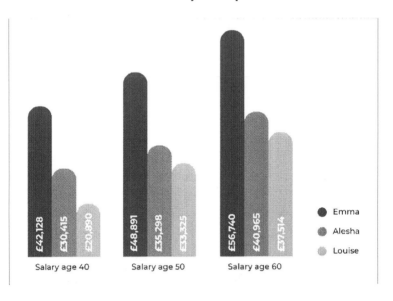

Figure 10. Real Life Case Study Salaries at Age 40, 50 and 60

Emma's salary is higher due to her promotions, which results in higher pension contributions, with a better compounding effect on her pension value — a real virtuous circle (see graph below).

Because Alesha's salary went backwards after her 2-year career break, this has a negative effect on her overall earnings and a negative compounding effect on her pension pot value.

The gap between her pension and Emma's in these real-life scenarios is now 23% compared to the previous 13%.

Louise's outcome is, not surprisingly, the worst. Because her long stint of part-time work has made it difficult for her to achieve the same level of full-time salary (maybe roles have changed in that 10 years, and the level of skill required to do the full-time job no longer matches what she can offer) the negative effect on her earnings (see above) also has a negative compounding effect on her pension pot value.

Base Case vs Real Life Pension Pot Value Age 60

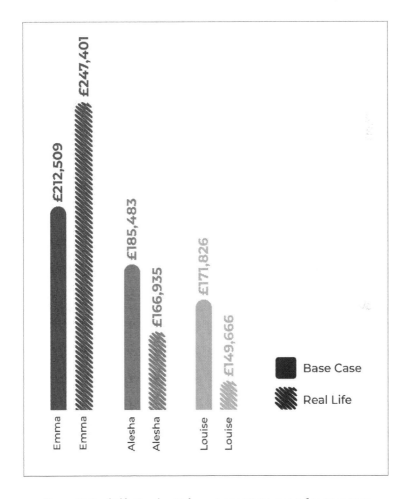

Figure 11. Real Life Pension Values at Age 60 Compared to Base Case

For Louise, working part-time until her child is at secondary school before reverting to full-time work has cost her dearly. Her pension pot is worth less than £150,000.

Although not as extreme, Alesha's decision to take a 2-year career break straight after giving birth has also financially disadvantaged her over the longer term. Her pension pot is worth £166,935 which is £18,500 less than the first scenario we looked at.

By contrast, Emma who has maintained full-time work has enjoyed the associated benefits of progressing her career via a couple of promotions, as well as maintaining full contributions into her pension each year.

Emma's pension is worth 65% more than Louise's by age 60, and 48% more than Alesha's, with a value of £247,401.

It may be easy to pick holes in these comparisons, but in real life, the situations of the women may diverge further if Alesha and Louise have more than one child and Emma only has one.

My point is that we don't think about the long-term. We focus on the short term and the effect of the decision on immediate household income. We just don't think about the effect that reduced pension contributions and compounding have over 30 years and where it will leave us financially in future.

In these scenarios for women earning £30,000 a year can result in future differences of nearly £100,000. Imagine the differences if you earn £50,000 or £60,000 a year before having children?

Evaluating the Options

I urge you to consider your long-term financial position seriously. To give it as much weighting and priority in your thinking and discussion with your partner as you do the well-being of your child. I think the knowledge and full appreciation of these facts is missing from the conversation between couples.

Your well-being is equally as important: both your long-term financial well-being and your shorter-term self-esteem and confidence in continuing to develop your career and maintaining your role as an income-earner.

Your identity as a mum will always be there throughout your life, but if you sacrifice too much of your financial identity, you may find it much harder in future to re-find yourself and re-create it.

> *If you sacrifice too much of your financial identity, you may find it much harder in future*

The snowball effect of these decisions is immense.

One solution when returning to work after maternity leave is to go back full-time, or as close to full-time as possible. This might be easier to do after the first baby than after subsequent ones, but that in itself will make a positive difference to your longer-term finances.

An enabler of this decision is to have the right childcare solution in place, whatever "right" means for you.

If you have a long commute to work, you might consider a more local job, to be closer to the nursery or childminder. Just consider carefully whether the role has the equivalent value, both financially and in terms of utilising your skills. A more local job is likely to pay a lower salary than the equivalent role in a city and is an underlying cause of the gender pay gap for women in their 30s.

The wider acceptance of homeworking post-Covid may go some way towards alleviating this situation, enabling you to return more easily to your original employer.

The affordability of childcare is also a key factor. Why not think of it as a shared or joint cost, not just a calculation of whether your salary when you return to work will cover it? This way of looking at it focuses all the responsibility on the mother's income which isn't fair.

Too often women say "by the time I've paid for child care and my travel costs, it's not worth me working." I would argue it is *always* worth you working.

> *I would argue it is always worth you working*

A simple agreement with your partner to say that his salary pays for the childcare, and your salary pays the mortgage, for example, puts a different perspective on the situation. It makes it feel more acceptable, more worthwhile and maintains the value of your earnings at the same level as his, rather than under-valuing your contribution.

As an aside, many larger companies offer Childcare vouchers which you or your partner may have the option to buy. This is a tax-advantaged method of paying for childcare which I urge you to do if it's available as an employee benefit.

Agreeing Your Return to Work

When thinking about my return to work after my second maternity leave in 2010, one of the mistakes I made (with the benefit of hindsight) was to accept that I needed to compromise on the hours I was paid to work, to achieve the flexibility I was looking for.

Not paying enough attention to the long-term financial implications of part-time working, which only now do I fully understand, I returned to work 4 days a week.

What I should have done was to agree on full-time working with full-time pay, but with flexibility on the hours I worked during the week.

For years I was paid for 4 days a week, when in fact the hours I was working and the results I delivered were equal to other colleagues working and being paid for full-time hours. This cost me about £150,000 in total remuneration (salary, bonus, car allowance) during those years and about £40,000 in future pension value. Very costly.

If I had my time again, this is something I would fight for, and I hope this will encourage you to do the same. Agreeing to a compressed hours contract, for example, in which you work full-time hours across 4 days a week, is now more widespread than it used to be.

Contracting With Your Partner

If you can find a way to return to work full-time, then the positive impact on your future earnings potential, on your long-term pension provision, and your sense of self-worth should be significant.

However, if that's not what you decide to do, and if you want to either stop working completely or reduce your hours, there are still steps you can take to reduce the negative financial impact for you.

One of the most important and simple things you can do is agree a contract with your partner to protect your future pension value.

If you jointly agree that you will give up or reduce your work, then also agree that he will continue to pay into your pension for you, at least matching what you were paying in, pre-children, ideally covering the employer contributions as well.

If it's not affordable to fully fund both his and your pension contributions from his salary, he may be able to reduce the contributions into his pension if he is currently paying in more than the minimum required. Any adjustment that can provide a fairer and more equitable approach to building your respective pensions is worth exploring and implementing.

This can be factored into the financial decision around starting a family, although financially there is often never a right time to start a family.

Maintaining pension provision for mums is something that the State already does.

During maternity leave and up until each child is aged 12, if you are registered to claim Child Benefit (whether or not you receive it), you receive a National Insurance credit each year towards your State Pension. You normally only pay National Insurance contributions (NICs) when you are earning an income and every year of contribution goes towards a year of State Pension. Throughout your adult life, you have to build up 35 years of NICs to be paid a full State Pension at your eligible age.

This credit arrangement means mums who are not working, or who are earning less than the NIC minimum threshold, can still accumulate State Pension benefits for the first 12 years of each child.

This is a positive mechanism to ensure that women who give up work to raise their children do not miss out on their entitlement to fair State Pension benefits in future.

Many women are unaware of this, and the key action here is to ensure that you register for Child Benefit, even if you are not eligible to receive it due to the high-income tax charge.

It's also important that it's you as the woman who registers, it shouldn't be your partner otherwise the benefit will not accrue to you.

So my suggestion is that we adopt this same principle and apply it to our personal or workplace pensions, even if household income is tight for a while.

> *The key action is to register for Child Benefit, even if you're not eligible to receive it*

It's important to take action to ensure financial fairness at the point you agree to change your working life, and not to assume it will happen later on if you separate or divorce.

Eyes Wide Open

There is a lot to take in and consider within this chapter. If my tone is more preachy and strident here, it just reflects how passionate I am about financial fairness for women and mums in particular.

Understanding this was my lightbulb moment. It's the culmination of my own experience as a working mum within the corporate workplace and my current knowledge of long-term financial planning.

Realising what a financial impact our decisions have on us decades later is a real eye-opener.

If you're in your 20s or 30s, you might still believe "it's such a long time in the future until I need to think about retiring, plenty of time to sort something out." If that's what you're thinking, please read Chapters 3 and 4 again!

Now that I am in my 50s and potentially only 10 years away from retiring, I would hate to be in a position of severely regretting the decisions I had taken when I was so much younger, even if they were with the best intentions and done from a position of wanting to be there for my baby or child when they were young.

My message is not that one path is right and the other wrong. However, I would encourage you to seriously consider returning to work full-time straight after maternity leave; it can be easier to balance work and childcare when the children are younger than it is when they start school.

If you decide *not* to return to work full-time, I recommend you:

1. Agree a contract with your partner that he will continue to fund your pension contributions, ideally at the same level as when you were working full-time.

2. If you are working part-time, allocate your income to cover household costs that are *not* the cost of child-care.

3. Consider learning a new skill or take an online qualification whilst raising the children — this will not only stimulate your mind but will keep your confidence and self-worth high.

4. Take the lead in managing your joint personal finances.

CHAPTER 6

Changing the Workplace

"Nothing is impossible. The word itself says 'I'm possible.'"

– Audrey Hepburn

In this chapter you will learn:

- why unfair situations remain which financially disadvantage women
- ideas to change and improve current workplace practices
- the critical role for senior female leaders in leading change

---

Workplaces have changed significantly over the decades in terms of culture, attitudes, behaviours and practices. They will continue to evolve as society changes, and whilst the direction of travel is positive, it takes time. Certain aspects are sometimes accelerated by pivotal moments and campaigns — recent examples of this being the Covid-19 experience and #metoo movement.

Looking back over my 30 years of work, whilst I see some progress and improvements — and am proud to have been a catalyst for change in the company I worked for — the pace of change overall feels slow. There are many opportunities to make quicker progress in several key areas, and for there to be a more consistent adoption of change across companies of all sizes.

Do We Get What We Deserve?

One of my main concerns is how embedded some of the progressive changes really are within a company's culture. Is it a living, breathing reality within the way an organisation conducts business or is it just written in a policy document in the CEO's or Head of HR's top drawer? Are many employers too often still saying one thing and doing another, following the path of least resistance?

Companies often talk about rewarding employees for results stating, "We are a results-driven organisation." However, this doesn't usually translate effectively into remuneration. Remuneration in terms of base salary continues to be driven by input rather than output. It's easier to measure someone's *quantity*, (the number of hours they work) than their *quality* (the effect of their work on the business results).

Even then, it's a flawed system because, in many roles and professions, employees work longer hours than they are contracted to, whether they are officially full-time or part-time. So in that context, no one is being paid fairly for the number of hours they work. The reality is often a combination of quantity and quality that is being remunerated.

So how is quality assessed in a company? We like to think it's based on contribution to results, skills demonstrated and perhaps future promotion potential. In reality though, other factors such as office politics, internal sponsorship and networking can all affect someone's career and remuneration.

In my corporate career, I shunned office politics and networking as I saw them as a 'boys' club' that I was excluded from. The classic formal networking activity was a corporate golf day, run by the Sales team with their retail and wholesale customers — at least 95% male every single year. No equivalent activity was ever run for women. Even now, I steadfastly refuse to play golf, just because of what it symbolises for me.

However, I didn't understand how important it was to build personal relationships within the company and how this would influence future decisions about my career.

> *The most important decisions about your career are taken when you're out of the room*

I recently listened to a speaker on International Women's Day saying "The most important decisions about your career are taken when you're out of the room. Therefore your representation in the room has to be strong." I wish I had understood this insight when I was in my 20s.

It's still a fact that the majority of senior managers responsible for making decisions about promotion and hiring are men.

We all instinctively act according to our self-image and we feel comfortable with people like ourselves. We believe we understand them and their motivations and behaviours, and therefore they are easier to get along with and manage. Of course, this is exactly why implementing a Diversity and Inclusion policy has to be a very conscious activity — we have to work hard to overcome the inbuilt biases which human nature has given us. We have to be active in seeking out people who are different to ourselves, will bring different experiences and perspectives, and be more reflective of the diverse customers and clients the company serves.

The same principles should be applied to women. Most men have never worked part-time, have never even considered the option. Most have never experienced the constant juggling of priorities, of having to leave work early for school pick-ups or at the drop of a hat when the school phones to say your child is ill, the constant guilt that many working mums feel, precisely because they are so loyal and conscientious towards their work, as well as to their children.

Speaking to an HR colleague recently, she said that men identify with, and define themselves, by their job more than women do. For example, when asked "what do you do for work?" a man is likely to say "I am a...business manager, sales director, IT consultant" whereas a woman will say "I work as a... business manager, in sales, in IT."

For women, their job is not who they are, it is what they do.

The reason for this is that women have multiple roles in their lives which they recognise and value, and they are not defined just by the work they do. I recognise this myself, even though I have already said how important my work is to me. I will often describe myself as a working mum. How many men describe themselves as working dads?

Maybe this difference is how men and women typically assess their roles in life, and at work, this should be more broadly understood and recognised? It doesn't necessarily indicate that a woman has less ambition or doesn't value her career potential as highly as a man. It's just different, and it requires insight and an open mind from a male boss to not automatically judge others against their own personally held unconscious belief system.

What's Causing the Gender Pay Gap?

Why does the gender pay gap still exist and what are the key contributing factors? We'll start with the good news that it is at least reducing.

For women in their 30s, the average pay gap now stands at 15.5%, according to Jane Portas' report - Living a financially resilient life in the UK beyond Covid-19, Nov 2020.

That's still a wide gap, however, and it increases after the age of 40. This is the time at which many women work part-time due to their family commitments or have gone back to work after an extended career break and are earning less. These figures are an average of an average, and ultimately what's important is your own experience and position.

I find it interesting that the reporting of the figures is automatically benchmarked against the average male salary.

There are different ways of reporting this same statistic. For example, if the average male salary is indexed at 100, it means the average female salary is 84 (after rounding).

However, if the average female salary is indexed at 100, it means the average male salary is 119. This means the *average male salary is 19% higher than the average female salary.*

Doesn't that make it sound more impactful, and more of an issue than saying "there is a pay gap of 15.5%?"

As referenced previously, Caroline Criado Perez has written a fascinating book called Invisible Women, about how data is used from a male perspective and creates an unconscious bias against women. I think the reporting of the gender pay gap is another example of how we continue to define problems from a male standpoint, even as we are trying to address them.

The reasons that cause the gender pay gap are complex. Nowadays it is not likely to be driven by a conscious decision to pay a woman less for doing the same job as a man. I'm not saying this never happens, but as it is now illegal to do so, it should never be as overt as this.

Let's examine some of the causes other than those already mentioned (part-time working, career breaks and working closer to home) that are relevant for all women in the workplace.

1. Self-Belief

Men and women behave differently in the workplace in respect of promotion and career progression. As a generalisation, men value their skills and their ability to do a great job more highly than women do. As one of my male bosses was fond of saying "don't let the facts get in the way of a good story."

I don't think this has changed much over the last 30 years, despite growing awareness and encouragement for women to understand this and to act differently. High profile women, such as Sheryl Sandberg with her book Lean In, have championed the need for women to promote themselves more effectively and negotiate harder for what they deserve, and I hope this has led to success for many women in the workplace.

However, it seems to me that we have been telling women for decades to value themselves more, to sell their skills and to put themselves forward for roles they may not feel qualified to do — in other words, to behave like men.

Men will typically have more confidence in their abilities, their skills, and the contribution they make to the company. They use this in many ways: as leverage to negotiate their salary, to negotiate their annual bonus, and to put themselves forward for promotion.

2. The Tiara Mentality

I think many women can relate to the idea that if you work hard and contribute to the success of your team or your company, you believe you will be recognised and rewarded. The expectation is that your boss will see this great work and think "she deserves a promotion."

But please be warned, particularly those of you in your 20s just starting your careers, this isn't usually true.

It's called the "tiara mentality." Women believe that someone will place a tiara on their heads in recognition of a job well done. A metaphorical "pat on the back" if you're a man.

You cannot take it for granted that what you do is being recognised and evaluated in the way you think it should.

If your male colleague in the team is also doing a great job, and he's telling his boss regularly about all the things he's doing and you're not doing the same, guess who's going to be top of the list for promotion?

It's not a simple as blaming your boss for not being fair or not being good at his or her job. It is not a conscious bias. The effect of someone telling you they're great when another person isn't doing the same, builds up over time. It can also be interpreted as someone keen to get on, compared to someone happy to stay where they are.

Women have to be able to market themselves, or perhaps sell themselves, to their bosses. They should be calling out all the personal contributions that have led to great outcomes for the business, listing the reasons why they deserve to be considered for that pay rise, or that promotion.

No one will manage your career for you, you have to do it yourself.

For women, this is often counter-intuitive to our biological nature

> *You cannot take it for granted that what you do is being recognised*

as carers or nurturers. We put others before ourselves. We are helpers and are therefore happy to help, to contribute for the good of the company or the greater cause. Maybe we don't expect to be rewarded monetarily, and guess what, if we act like this then we won't be.

3. Pay and Reward Structures

The gender pay gap can start at the very beginning of men and women's careers, driven by their choice of profession or job, with many male-dominated professions paying much higher salaries: think investment banking, IT, engineering compared to nursing and primary school teaching.

Also, when comparing like for like within the same profession, the gap can start to open quickly.

Your entry point salary is crucial, as is the first promotion you receive. If the company you work for is open to having salary negotiated, and most are, men are more likely to be successful in this than women. We used to believe that men were more proactive in asking for, and negotiating salary increases, but more recent research suggests this isn't the whole picture. Women are now more likely than previously to be asking for salary increases but are less likely to be successful in being awarded one[1].

Standard HR remuneration practice for annual salary reviews and promotions is to apply an agreed % to a basic salary. The manager promoting you will have visibility of your current pay and will almost certainly decide on your new salary with that as the starting point, rather than thinking "this job is worth a salary of £x."

Due to this practice of incrementalism, if a woman starts her career in the early years being paid less than an equivalent male colleague, the compounding effect of that early gap on her career earnings will be significant. And what starts as a small gap becomes a larger one over time.

Let's look at an example in which two people have a £2,000 difference in their base salary. Let's see the effect of a 5% pay rise each year over ten years.

If Jane has a salary of £30,000, then after 10 years of successive pay rises, her salary becomes £48,867. If Paul has a salary of £32,000, after 10 years of successive pay rises, his salary is £52,125.

What starts as a £2,000 difference becomes a £3,258 difference after 10 years.

Paul & Jane's Salary Difference Over 10 Years

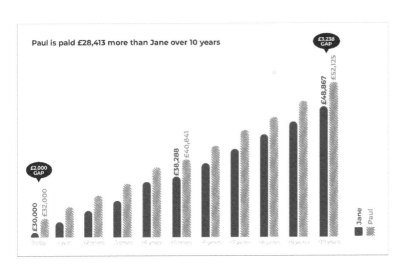

Figure 12. Example of Salary Differences Over 10 Years

This salary difference affects their pay every single year. This means that over ten years, Paul is paid £28,413 more than Jane, not to mention being paid higher bonuses and receiving higher pension contributions.

Is that fair, if they are doing the same role? I think not.

Other remuneration practices within the workplace also reflect and reward the typical financial journey of a man's career. For example, career longevity or length of service is usually valued and often financially rewarded. This can come in the form of share options after a certain number of years worked, additional holiday days, or still the traditional carriage clock or cufflinks.

Another example I have seen with some of my clients' employers is a particular reward that's driven by the age you are within a company. The older you are and the closer to retirement age you are, the higher pension contribution you receive as a % of your salary.

This is a great benefit if you have worked for that company for many years, have a high level of earnings due to many years of inflationary pay rises, and are still employed by them in your 50s and 60s. Fantastic.

But these examples discriminate indirectly against women who are less likely to have continuous years of long service with one company due to taking career breaks, and when they have re-entered the workplace, their earnings are likely to be lower.

Of course, this is also the case for women working part-time. So even those women who can benefit from higher pension contributions in their 50s and 60s, are likely to be on a lower salary than their equivalent male peers.

In its Insuring Women's Futures Manifesto, authored by Jane Portas, the Chartered Insurance Institute is calling for companies to publish their pension contribution data by gender, as well as salary by gender. This is to highlight the issue of the gender pensions gap.

Having worked in the area of diversity for several years, the question of measures, quotas, and targets is always controversial, but there is a truth that what gets measured gets done.

So I am in favour of reporting these statistics. Solutions for reducing any gaps are then down to the individual company. It's for them to understand which of their Pay & Reward practices contribute most to the figures and re-think them through a gender-neutral lens to make them fair for women as well as men.

Levelling the Playing Field

Permanent change to address the ways men and women are assessed and treated differently in the workplace can only be embedded within a company through its culture. Culture is the way all employees think and act within a company to get business done. It reflects the values of the company and what's important to the company in how it operates.

Any change of culture or adoption of a new value requires emotional engagement and acceptance throughout the organisation. This needs to start from the top of the company and cascade down, touching all departments and all aspects of work done. It needs to be business-led, not seen as an HR initiative. Otherwise, it won't have staying power.

Most if not all larger companies have a documented Diversity & Inclusion strategy which they claim guides how they operate.

I challenge you to really scrutinise the culture of the company you currently work for and assess what they do well in this area, and what can be improved. If you have any personal experiences or issues as a result of being female, then the D&I strategy is either not fit for purpose or is not being implemented effectively.

Exercise:

Let's consider an example of culture and one of the key inflection points for women in their lives – whether to move away from the norm of full-time working once they've had a child.

How is flexible and part-time working viewed and implemented in your company?

Is it willingly offered?

Are the part-time roles as challenging and contributory to the business as full-time roles?

Are full-time colleagues supportive of part-time workers or are there 'jokes' made about slacking off or leaving early?

Ultimately, the question is:

Are part-time or flexible roles commanding the same status as full-time roles in your organisation?

If you think the answer is no, this is a good place to start the conversation with the leadership team and colleagues.

Many working mums do not want to compromise their career and don't want their desire for a more flexible working arrangement to be interpreted as a signal that they are less ambitious than before they had children. However, they also may not want to conform to the increasingly outdated concept of working Monday to Friday 9 am to 5 pm.

There's a great book called The 100-Year Life written by Lynda Gratton and Andrew Scott. They detail the social history of paid work when it used to be an activity every single day, then became 6 days a week in the industrialised era, then reduced to 5 days, where it has remained for many decades. Who's to say the norm couldn't be 4 days a week in future?

In terms of flexible location, I truly hope that the working-from-home (WFH) experience, created by Covid-19, has accelerated the acceptance of this practice amongst senior leaders who were previously non-believers. I hope that as many working dads as mums have experienced the benefits of being able to do the school run, going out for a run or walk, and generally being trusted to manage their own time whilst still getting their job done well.

Breaking the taboo of presenteeism in the office is a significant breakthrough. However, if hybrid working becomes the new normal, or if some employees continue to WFH permanently, it means that managers will have to work a little harder to get to know their WFH team members just as well as they know those who come into the office. Otherwise, this could create a 2-tier system that might end up discriminating against women.

This concern has been voiced to me by one of my clients, a female Chief Operating Officer. She worries that, over time, the mixture of remote and office working might create differences in behaviour between men and women. Will men return to the office in higher numbers than women, who are still likely to be taking the lead with parallel family commitments alongside their work? Will men have more visibility in the office than women, resulting unconsciously in more promotional opportunities for men?

This is something we must all be conscious of and try to avoid. If you and your partner both work in an office environment, maybe you can continue to share the flexible practice of working from home rather than one being in the office more than the other? If enough couples commit to doing this, it could be very influential.

Ideas for Change: Evolution Not Revolution

What practical steps can we take to influence change bottom-up and to drive change top-down in our workplaces?

1. Make Part-Time Roles Sexy

Part-time working is still seen as the province of women and in particular working mums. What we once hailed as a breakthrough in women's rights now has the potential to hold back women's careers, as the uptake of flexible working by men has been so low.

When I was considering my own situation and whether to return to work full-time or part-time, I discussed the part-time option with several colleagues at the company. If I worked fewer than five days a week, would this send a different signal to the bosses about my level of ambition for my future career? Would it change the perception of the level of competence and skills I had?

When men are asked why they do not work part-time, they generally share the same concern as women, namely the impact that part-time work is likely to have on their careers.

The real issue is that part-time roles are often lower-skilled, or perceived to have lower status than their equivalent full-time roles. Creating reduced-hour roles that have a contributory status to the business equal to full-time roles would produce a motivated workforce in which everyone's full potential and skillsets can be utilised, regardless of the number of days they work.

It would give the employer a great edge over its competition to attract and retain the best talent.

Creating challenging, interesting and career-progressing part-time roles has proven too much for many companies. I believe there is a certain laziness in the corporate workplace and that much more could be done to design roles at all levels that are strategic contributors to a company's results, whether done 3 days, 4 days or 5 days a week.

And whatever happened to job-share? There are certain industries such as the teaching profession and other public sector roles in which job share is very common, yet it's not such common practice within the private sector.

A 6-month project, with help from external consultants, could redesign significant parts of an organisation to achieve this, particularly for office-based work. Adopting best practices from within the public sector could be a real opportunity.

2. Assess Skills, Not Experience

When a company first takes on school leavers and graduates, it often follows an in-depth process to evaluate the skills, personal qualities and career potential of the candidates. The various rounds of tests, online response interviews and assessment centres that my son went through when applying for jobs after University was mind-blowing.

When a graduate is entering the workplace for the first time, their past work experience is, by definition, limited and therefore largely irrelevant to the employer. What the employer is looking for instead are the skills, personal qualities and motivation from the individual to succeed.

Why is this same approach to assessment not continued within the workplace when people are assessed for their leadership potential and future promotion?

A rigorous approach to skills assessment can make any past experience less important, and instead can focus on whether an individual is capable of succeeding in a more responsible role.

> *A rigorous approach to skills assessment can make past experience less important*

This feels like a much fairer way of evaluating people's potential. It can remove the issue of whether someone has or is working reduced hours, whether they took 6 months or 12 months maternity leave, or potentially an even longer career break.

It must be possible to design a set of tests, activities and scenarios to evaluate skills objectively when promoting into key leadership roles.

One of the things we used to do at my previous company once a year was a full-blown crisis management simulation. It was run by an external company, carefully designed with input from the senior leadership team to replicate a potential real-life crisis for the company. That sorted the wheat from the chaff!

Why could such a thing not be used effectively to assess the potential of individuals as future leaders? This could create a much more level playing field, not only for women but for other minority groups who also struggle to compete fairly with the white male status quo.

This approach can break the chain of promotion being based largely on time spent and experience gained within previous roles, as opposed to true skill and capability.

3. Embrace Skills and Knowledge Gained Outside the Workplace

Companies also need to scrutinise how they value skills and knowledge that have not been gained in the workplace. I'm specifically referring to the skills gained by women during maternity leave.

This is a time when women can often feel they have fallen behind whilst being away from work, and it makes them feel on the back foot.

But ladies, whilst you've been at home raising a small child, you have developed skills that are hugely valuable within the workplace. You can now multitask with ease. You can prioritise and make quick decisions at the drop of a hat. You know how precious your time is so you are ultra-efficient when it comes to fitting all of the priorities and tasks into your day. These are skills that any employer should be valuing hugely.

I know several mums who used their maternity leave to study and learn new skills, and yet these were dismissed by their employer when returning to work.

When returning to work after maternity leave or a career break, wouldn't it be refreshing for the conversation with your manager to start with "so tell me all the new skills you've developed whilst on maternity leave, and how you think these will benefit our company?" Compare this to starting with "well, you've been out of the workforce for 12 months now so you're probably feeling a bit rusty, and a lot has changed since you've been away, so you'll have to catch up."

You have the opportunity to control this conversation, and by preparing well for those discussions before re-entering the workplace, you can greatly influence how you are perceived and valued on your return.

4. Mentor All New Entrants

A good, low-cost idea is to have in place a mentoring programme for all new entrants to a company. I believe this will particularly benefit women, although there will be potential benefits for all.

Providing young women entering the workplace with a more senior female mentor, to share their wisdom and the lessons they have learned, could make a real difference to that young woman's career. They can point out the realities of needing to manage yourself and your career, the importance of networking to build relationships as widely as possible and coaching on how best to approach new job and promotion opportunities.

New entrants are likely to be optimistic, enthusiastic, and by definition naive about office politics. Let's prevent history repeating itself over and over again, with young women expecting that their line manager will recognise, reward and promote them automatically if they do a good job. Far better to make them aware right upfront of the realities, to avoid disappointment and disillusionment in future if they feel they have not been treated or evaluated fairly in comparison to their male colleagues.

Skills training for all new entrants in how to present themselves and their achievements constructively in appraisals and performance reviews would also be a positive step.

5. Say "No" to Salary Negotiation

I want to return to the subject of salary because *the money really matters.*

Money creates choices and options and can bolster self-worth when you feel your contribution is being fairly recognised and rewarded.

Rather than an incremental process, I believe the start point should be, what is fair pay for a person with these skills doing this job?

I understand that companies are commercial enterprises looking to make a profit. I am a business owner and employer myself. But there is a balance to strike. It is a moral responsibility of any company to pay all their employees fairly, whether the company is big or small.

Let's take the salary out of the hiring or promotion decision and make it non-negotiable.

Why *should* pay be negotiable?

If someone tries to negotiate, the answer can simply be, "no, this is the salary we are paying for this role." It's a take it or leave it situation. In a world in which women are less likely to negotiate their salary successfully compared to men, this is a big step towards creating a fairer playing field.

This policy would specifically support women returning to the workplace after maternity leave or a career break, and who may not feel in a position of strength to negotiate their salary.

In Chapter 7, I take the idea further, to make salary a protected characteristic, so it would be illegal for an employer to ask what someone's previous or current salary is.

Many companies operate salary bands. And the argument in favour of having some flexibility around awarding pay rises is that it gives employers the ability to increase somebody's pay within a band as their experience and skills develop. I think that's a reasonable procedure and there's no reason why this would need to change, as long as the range of salary within a band is narrow. If it's too wide then, again, over time and longevity of service, it has the effect of creating a widening gender pay gap.

Employers also need to retain mechanisms for differentiating between excellent, average and poor performance within roles, but this doesn't necessarily need to be done financially, via a bonus or salary (which increases pensionable earnings and thereby also the monetary value of pension contributions – a double benefit).

There are many non-financial ways of rewarding top-performers or those who exceed their objectives in any given year. Vouchers for holidays, weekends away, gift experiences, fine dining, concert and theatre vouchers — it's an endless list that can be scaled up or down in monetary value. It just takes some thought and creativity to make it work, rather than defaulting to a base salary increase.

6. Appoint a Remuneration Tsar

Talking with female senior leaders, many recognise pay negotiation and salary increases as a challenge within their own companies.

One way to manage these issues is to ensure consistent application of practices, such as "no negotiation," and to prevent unconscious bias in promotion decisions by creating a specific role within the company to oversee it.

The Remuneration Tsar is a senior director with a business or operational background rather than HR, who assesses every proposed pay rise, promotion or hiring decision with the relevant team manager. They ensure that no gender bias or other indirect discrimination creeps in, that all managers adopt the same approach to pay, and that male employees aren't negotiating their pay to a higher level than their female peers.

An alternative idea to one individual having this role is to form a small sub-committee of 3 Directors or C-suite representatives to perform the same function.

What gets measured gets done.

This would be a powerful signal for a company to send to its employees; that the implementation of their Diversity and Inclusion policy, which has fair pay and fair career opportunity at its heart, is not being left to chance but is being actively managed across the organisation.

7. Establish a Gender Diversity Workgroup

I ran a Gender Diversity workstream across Europe on behalf of my company (alongside my day job of course!) and I enlisted the support of like-minded women, across all the countries, keen to see changes. We worked as a virtual team, researching the grass-roots issues, agreeing on the scope of our work and our objectives.

We ultimately changed the culture and practice around flexible working, not just within the UK, but in Spain, Italy, and many countries where local management was sceptical about it at the outset.

We achieved this because our initiatives were sponsored by the European senior leadership team, which all country managers were a member of. They knew that an effective and motivated female workforce was instrumental in them achieving the best business results. Their vocal and practical support and then leadership of implementing change was crucial.

Exercise:

- Make a short list of the two or three most relevant areas you would like to see change in the company you work for.

- What facts do you know, and what areas need more exploration?

- How can you gather more insight, feedback and evidence?

- If you could change one thing within your organisation to make it fairer for women, what would it be?

Culturally, it's important that fresh ideas are encouraged and welcomed into the business. Not all of them may ultimately be appropriate or practical, but the very act of considering alternatives, debating options and engaging senior leaders should lead to positive change.

Download this exercise at: www.dare2befair.com

It all starts with understanding the main issues or blocks being experienced throughout the organisation, whether there are 20, 200 or 2,000 employees.

Being Fair

This chapter has covered a lot of topics and ideas. You may feel differently about your ability to influence these areas within your organisation, depending on how junior or senior you are.

But as I hope I have made clear, change can and should be stimulated both bottom-up and top-down. Good ideas can come from anywhere, and often externally to a company. Getting a better understanding of what's happening in other companies, other industries, sectors, or countries will all be useful.

Returning to the financial theme, let's remember the central, fundamental importance of ensuring that women are remunerated fairly in salary, bonus and pension contributions, that they have equal access to promotional opportunities and career development to ensure a fair financial future.

If you're reading this as a senior manager in your company, please reflect on your own career journey, and evaluate any points at which you questioned if you were being paid or treated fairly.

You are the ones who are best placed to change culture and practices more quickly through a top-down approach.

Be courageous, intelligent and strategic as you approach these challenges — and you can achieve great things.

CHAPTER 7

Will Society Dare To Be Fair?

*"Alone we can do so little; together we can
do so much."*

— **Helen Keller**

In this chapter you will learn:

- the evolution of women's rights in relation to financial and social independence from men
- ideas for changing legislation and government policy to support women returning to work
- how you can help create change via your friends, networks and social media

The Evolution of Change

Women have had to fight for their rights on many occasions over the last 100 years. There has been a gradual evolution of change regarding women's status in society, moving towards a more equitable status alongside men.

This timeline shows a lot of the key changes that occurred, but many didn't happen without years of protest and lobbying. We have to fight for fairness as it's a man's world, designed through the eyes of men who have only their own experiences to draw on.

We have to continue to point out the areas in which we are still falling short of being fair to women.

Legislative Milestones for Women and Emancipation Over the Past 100 Years in the UK

Year	Act	Description
1918	Representation of the People Act[1]	Enabled women over 30 who met certain property qualifications to vote. This meant that two-thirds of UK women could vote, although large discrepancies between men and women's voting rights remained.[2]
	Parliament (Qualification of Women) Act	Removed the disqualification of women from parliament through sex and marriage. There were no age restrictions on women standing for Parliament.[3]
1920	Sex Disqualification (Removal Act)	Prohibited people being disqualified from the legal profession, civil service and accountancy on account of their sex.[4]
1923	Matrimonial Causes Act	Gave spouses equal rights in initiating a divorce.[5]
1925	Law of Property Act	Created equality between spouses with respect to inheriting property.[6]
1928	Equal Franchise Act	All women over 21 could vote, giving them the same voting rights as men.[2]
1941	National Service Act	Introduced conscription for women. All unmarried women and widows aged 20-30 without children could be called up for service.
1946	The National Health Service Act	Prior to the introduction of the NHS, only insured persons could readily access health care, and men were disproportionately insured compared to women.[1]
1956	Civil Service (Equal Pay)	Created equal pay between the genders for civil servants and teachers.[7]
1958	Life Peerages Act	Enabled women to sit in the House of Lords.
1964	Married Women's Property Act	Entitled a wife to have joint ownership over housekeeping money with her husband.[6]
	Abortion Act	Legalised abortion on certain grounds.[9]

1967	National Health Service (Family Planning) Act	Made contraception readily available to many more women.[10]
1970	Equal Pay Act	Banned employers from giving women less favourable working conditions or lower pay than men, largely in response to the strikes by women at the Ford car site in Dagenham in 1968.[1]
1975	Sex Discrimination Act	Allowed married women to open a bank account in their name without requiring their husband's permission.[1]
1975	Employment Protection Act	Made it illegal to fire a woman for being pregnant and introduced statutory maternity provision.[1]
1976	Domestic Violence and Matrimonial Proceedings Act	Introduced legal protection for women and children who were being domestically abused.[12]
1985	Equal Pay (Amendment) Act	Cited that women should be paid the same as men for work of equal value.[1]
1986	Sex Discrimination (Amendment) Act	Allowed women to retire at the same age as men and to work during the night in factories.[1]
1988	1988 Budget	Nigel Lawson introduced independent taxation between spouses. From 1990, a wife was taxed as an individual earner, not as if her income was a part of her husband's.[13]
1991	R v R	The landmark House of Lords case made marital rape illegal.[14]
1998	Human Rights Act	Incorporated the principles established in the European Convention of Human Rights into UK law.
1999	The Maternity and Parental Leave Regulations	Enabled men and women to take time off work to look after young children.[15]
2003	Section 28 was repealed from the Local Government Act 1988	Repealing Section 28 helped create greater gender and sexual equality.[16]
2014	The Shared Parental Leave Regulations 2014	Allowed mothers to transfer some of their maternity leave to their partner.[17]

Figure 13. Legislative Milestones for Women and Emancipation Over the Past 100 Years in the UK

We still witness and experience examples of injustice and unfairness, so we need to keep pushing forwards. To create change, we need to influence:

- at a personal level, through our friends and social networks both in person and online
- at a corporate level, stimulating bottom-up influence from all employees and top-down change led by senior managers
- at a legislative level, lobbying for government policy to create legislation that will enforce changes in the workplace and society

No significant shift happens quickly, but things can and do change when there are enough voices, enough focus and enough practical ways of implementing the change.

We just need to consider the last 100 years to acknowledge the positive direction of travel and have the courage to know that change can continue. We can reduce the number of women retiring in poverty and create better financial futures for women across society.

How Much Does Society Value Mums?

One of the greatest challenges to address, I think, is society's attitude towards mums and the issue of working versus not working.

How does society value the role of women in giving birth and raising children? Very highly, one would have to say. Of course, this is a female's biological role and is still regarded as the priority role for women, to greater or lesser degrees across different cultures, religions and societies.

In our Western culture, society promotes a wider remit for women than just raising children, but as the timeline shows, the shift towards women being financially independent of men — as money-earners, land and business-owners, employers etc. — is still relatively recent.

It's shocking to realise that many financial practices have only moved out of male control in very recent history. It was only in 1975 that married women could have a personal bank account without needing their husband's permission. Up until 1985, it was still legal for a woman to be paid less than a man for the same work. It wasn't until the early 1990s that a married woman was considered a financially independent person, separate from her husband, in terms of income and taxation.

As we're now in an era where sexual harassment and violence is being called out and addressed, we need to simultaneously keep shining a light on the financial vulnerability of many women.

Whoever controls the money, controls the relationship.

If you don't have your own money or assets, you are particularly vulnerable to poverty, especially in the later years of your life.

Although society may value women's childbearing role highly, it can lead to financial dependence and therefore disadvantage for women. The value of this role to society has never been monetised. By that I mean, there has never been a monetary value put on the time, skills and effort spent by women on raising children.

If you were employed and paid to have children, how much would it be worth? £20,000 a year? £30,000 a year? It could be anything. Ultimately it's invaluable to society because if women stopped giving birth, life as we know it would stop.

Yet, in monetary terms, women in the UK are penalised and disadvantaged for performing this vital role in society. Their long-term financial security and resilience remain locked together with those of their partner (if they have one) or, if they are single mothers, they have only themselves and a limited amount of state support to draw from.

If Mother Nature had determined that men could give birth as well as women, what do you think the level of maternity pay and financial support would be? My bet is it would be massively different to what is on offer today.

Financial Support for Women Returning to Work

One of the key ideas I want to champion is for the state to support working mums much more at the point when they return to work.

The value and benefit to both the employer and the mum of returning to the workplace as soon as appropriate after giving birth is significant. With a maternity leave of say, 6-9 months, the mum will retain her work knowledge, her skill level, and very importantly, her confidence.

Therefore, she is at her *most valuable* to the employer if she returns to work after a shorter period of maternity leave than someone who has a longer period of absence from the workplace.

She may also not have missed an annual pay rise or promotion opportunity, thereby maintaining her financial security and future earnings potential, compared to a longer career break which might not allow for this continuity.

Confidence, knowledge and skill level can all deteriorate over time. If a woman waits two, three or ten years before returning to the workplace, she may well feel like a different person and doubt her competency and capability by that stage. It means that she may just feel grateful for being offered any job, and possibly end up in a role where she is underutilised and underpaid relative to her skills.

Yet there is no financial incentive in place within the State Benefits system: no income tax break for working mums, no free childcare until the child is aged three.

I've outlined the financial benefits of returning to work, after maternity leave, full-time or as close to full-time as possible, taking advantage of the now more widely accepted option of flexible hours and flexible location. But the one thing that would make this option much more viable and affordable for many families would be if some form of state-sponsored financial support was available.

Why not have an income tax break for women who return to work to help them cover the cost of childcare, whether that be at a nursery, paying grandparents, a nanny or a childminder?

This could be in place for a number of years after the birth of a child and then gradually reduced down to normal levels of income taxation. If this enables women to earn higher salaries and have longer careers, the tax relief will be recovered through higher income tax receipts, and the country's productivity and the economy will increase.

When I researched "tax breaks for working mums to encourage them to return to work," the most recent news articles I could find were dated 2013 and 2014. Somehow this debate seems to have gone quiet.

In an article in The Spectator in 2014, there is a coherent case for the economic benefits of having more mums at work. It also states that there are 2.4 million British mums who want to work but don't, and a further 1.3 million who work part-time but can't afford to do more hours. This is because the UK has amongst the highest childcare costs in the world as well as prohibitively stringent regulations related to childcare provision.

One way of implementing financial support is to make the cost of childcare fully tax-deductible i.e. paid without being taxed or subject to national insurance contributions. This would significantly reduce the amount you need to earn to pay for the childcare, or conversely, means you have a lot more money available in your salary each month after paying for the childcare.

This makes the financial equation of returning to work stack up much more favourably.

If you earn £50,000 a year and your childcare costs £1,000 a month, so £12,000 a year, you have to earn just under £18,000 of taxable income to pay for it (once income tax and NI have been deducted).

If you are a higher rate taxpayer you have to earn even more to fund the childcare, due to higher tax rates.

An income tax break or relief in which no tax is applied would mean that £12,000 childcare requires £12,000 from your gross salary, which would save working parents thousands of pounds each year.

A similar approach can be applied to paying for a nanny. Almost a third of the cost of a nanny is accounted for in various taxes. Without these, work would become more viable for thousands of women, according to The Spectator, and would also create demand for many more nannies.

In other countries, the cost of childcare is heavily subsidised by the government. For example, the Norwegian government heavily subsidises both public and private day-care centres, making headlines in 2012 when the maximum amount paid by parents for childcare was NOK 2,330 (£252) per month.

In Sweden, the Parental Leave System has enabled more equality between men and women to take maternity/paternity leave, resulting in an employment rate of mothers of children less than 7 years old, among the highest among OECD countries[18].

Let's encourage our MPs to think creatively about how government can provide financial support to women at this critical decision point, this Moment That Matters[19], when they are making their decision to return to work.

Where there's a political will, there's a way.

Protecting Salary Information When Hiring

The second area of legislative change I want to explore is making it illegal for employers to ask a candidate applying for a job to quote their current or previous pay. The issue with this practice is it provides a benchmark from which the employer can apply an incremental increase, as explored in the previous chapter.

Making salary a 'protected characteristic', in HR speak, would operate in the same way as the other personal details a hiring employer is no longer able to ask about: age, sexual orientation, whether they intend to have children, for example.

Taking salary out of the hiring decision means that a robust job description is required, with all of the skills and qualities listed for somebody who would be successful in that role.

Undoubtedly this will make it more challenging for employers but many already benchmark similar roles across their industry, so they know what a fair salary looks like for specific roles.

This will make the hiring process fairer for women re-entering the workplace, by ensuring that the salary offered for the new role is not pegged at a lower level than is appropriate, because of their previous earnings.

If combined with employers not allowing candidates to negotiate the advertised salary, it creates a strong position that the employer controls whilst being equitable for all candidates and new entrants.

Over time it should result in everyone, not just women, being paid fairly, according to their skills and what they bring to the job, as opposed to just an increment of a previous salary.

The Right to Challenge Fair Pay

Labour MP Stella Creasey has put forward proposed legislation called the Equal Pay Information and Claims Bill 2020. It had its first reading in the House of Commons in October 2020. In Stella's speech during this first reading, she explained the key provisions as:

- seeks to make pay more transparent
  - Without transparency, women can never know if they are being paid fairly.
  - This will also help to tackle the pay gap between different ethnicities.
  - It is based on the principle that even if women are just as likely as men to ask for a pay rise, employers are more likely to listen to men.
- expanding gender pay gap reporting to organisations with 100 or more employees
- introducing ethnic pay reporting: companies with more than 100 employees to produce annual reports on their ethnic pay gap

The economic benefits of tackling the gender pay gap are huge. Stella said in her speech, "The Bank of England forecasts that ending the gender pay gap would add £600 billion to our economy by 2025, and ending discrimination against those from black and ethnic minority backgrounds in the workplace, would add £24 billion a year to our GDP."

Challenges remain in getting this legislation heard, debated and ultimately passed. Stella Creasey is a Labour MP and non-government sponsored, private member bills are more likely to fail due to lack of parliamentary time. However, there is cross-party support for the bill and it is sponsored in the House of Lords by Baroness Margaret Prosser, a key supporter of such reforms and a champion of equal pay.

The timeframe remains lengthy, and whilst I welcome this initiative to create more transparency and therefore accountability, I feel in some ways it is locking the door after the horse has bolted.

It aims to report on existing pay gaps and problems rather than introducing legislation that may *improve* the situation. However, I recognise that if employers know they may be called to account in this area by an employee, it may result in fairer practices across the board.

If a female or ethnic minority employee needs this legislation to have transparency of their pay compared to colleagues because they have a strong suspicion it's not fair, then the employer has already morally failed. It indicates a culture of unfairness that is endemic within the company.

As outlined in the previous chapter, maybe what large organisations need is a Remuneration Tsar to ensure a company is proactively staying on the right side of fairness?

Other Change Initiatives

There are additional well-researched and formulated initiatives being championed by the Chartered Insurance Institute (CII) and other organisations and individuals.

One of these is extending gender pay gap reporting to include gender pension contribution gap reporting. The purpose of this is to highlight the differences between pension contributions being made by employers for men and women.

Another initiative is making it the default that pensions are shared as assets in a divorce, which is not currently the case.

I strongly support this initiative. Up to 70% of divorces do not incorporate pension sharing[20]. This would make a monumental difference to so many divorcing women, who are usually the financially weaker party. It will particularly benefit women who do not work with a solicitor during their divorce.

I urge all Family Law solicitors to continue focusing on pensions within the divorce settlements they negotiate for their female clients, and to work with Financial Planners to accurately understand the future position at retirement, to achieve a fair share of pension value at the point of divorce.

Specific groups and alliances already campaigning and lobbying for reform in these and similar areas include:

- **Women's Equality Party**:
  Co-founded in 2016 by Sandi Toksvig and Catherine Mayer.
  www.womensequality.org.uk
  #enoughisenough

- **The Fawcett Society:**

  Campaigning for gender equality and women's rights at work, at home and in public life.

  www.fawcettsociety.org.uk

Many of the large financial institutions (banks, wealth managers) also have campaigns designed to reach out to women to equalise access and participation in financial matters.

There may be a cause that you feel you would like to join and lend your voice and support to.

I have recently become an ambassador for Insuring Women's Futures, a programme hosted by the Chartered Insurance Institute, which is committed to improving the resilience of women's financial futures. There are more details of materials authored by Jane Portas in the Resources section.

Inspiring Your Friends

If political campaigning isn't your bag, something you can do at a much more personal and local level is to tap into your strong female and social networks.

You can talk to friends about the issues and consequences high-lighted in this book and encourage debate around them.

You can help break the taboo of talking about money and get the conversation flowing more freely, a conversation from which we can all learn and educate ourselves, as well as discussing what's best to do in our own lives.

We know as women just how important and influential our female friends are throughout our lives, particularly when we are facing problems or have big decisions to make. Becoming a mum for the first time is usually made so much more enjoyable, and survivable, with the support of a mums' network.

Research by Lloyds Bank in 2019 found that 50% of UK adults believe that talking about personal money matters is taboo.

Why is it that women do not talk as freely about money as other subjects with their friends?

Maybe it's due to concern over not wishing to appear wealthier than friends, or conversely not wanting to feel inferior if money is tight. Maybe it's through fear of embarrassing somebody else within the group by talking about money.

But money is the means to an end. Money gives you choices and can enable you to achieve your future goals.

I believe we should be talking a lot more about the importance of planning financially for our future, starting when we are single, independent women. A good conversation starter could be talking about what your own childhood experiences of money were, how your parents were with money — some of the considerations and questions detailed in Chapter 2 about women's money mindsets. It doesn't all have to be about what we earn and how much we spend each month.

There is also much to do in schools, to equip both boys and girls with knowledge to enable them to manage their finances effectively as adults.

The importance of women getting themselves personally involved in their finances — right now, and for their future benefit – should be shouted from the rooftops!

Please use my Instagram account @dare2befair to let me know which areas you find women are most open to discussing, which ones they shy away from, which ones resonate most and seem the most important.

Pick Your Cause

In summary, think about how best you can make your own voice heard. What ideas do *you* have? What causes or issues resonate with you most? Where do you feel you can have the most influence?

Please get involved, whether:

- it's at a personal level, sorting out your financial situation, working with a financial planner to help you achieve the best possible future, and encouraging your female friends to do the same

- you're inspired to constructively challenge your employer and organisation to make some important changes, which will open up fairer pay and career opportunities than is currently the case

- you want to lobby your MP or join a political party to create social and legislative change

We need women acting and influencing at all levels to create a fairer future for ourselves and for those who will follow us.

We need to stop women from retiring in poverty, with only 20% of the pension wealth of men. We have to challenge ourselves, our employers and our society to Dare To Be Fair.

Closing Thoughts:
Time to Act

I hope you have found the ideas in this book thought-provoking.

I hope you have taken on board some of the financial realities that I have outlined.

I hope you feel inspired to get involved in your finances, and not to be daunted, or overwhelmed by the thought of investing. It is a straightforward activity when done correctly.

My Manifesto

Drawing all the themes and ideas within the book together results in one key rallying cry:

Get Involved!

- Improve things for yourself, at a personal level.
- Improve things in the workplace, for you and those who come after you.
- Improve things through societal change and legislation.

Strive to be financially self-sufficient.

Creating change is a long process, but it's often created from a series of little actions that build and expand, and if enough people talk and then act, it becomes a movement.

Eventually, the lawmakers catch up and new legislation can embed change for the good of all.

If changing the world is not your bag, then start at home, literally.

Get involved in planning your finances for the long-term as well as the short-term.

Talk to your partner in order to make joint decisions about your shared future, for your children and for the life you want in retirement.

Make sure your future pension will give you the money you need to live a great life in retirement.

Be prepared and ready for the fact that life may throw curveballs — health, relationships, work — all of these are more fragile than we often realise.

The more you know about your financial situation, the more you can navigate through the changes that come your way.

Think very carefully about your work and family decisions when having children.

Strive to work full-time after maternity leave.

Share the benefits, and greater opportunity, of flexible working with your partner, so that you can both pursue your careers, for personal fulfilment as well as financial benefits.

Shine a light on your employer's workplace practices and culture.

Identify areas where change needs to occur and set about making that change happen.

The more senior you are, the more influence you have. Use it wisely and proactively, and leave a legacy that you are proud of.

Support and improve the financial rewards and career progression of women in your organisation.

Some change requires new laws to embed and enforce it.

Let's campaign to make pay a protected characteristic and for working mums to pay no income tax on their childcare when they return to work.

Talk to your friends.

Raise the volume and quality of debate around personal finances.

Let's stop the many financial disadvantages for women that are systemic in the way we currently think and act.

Whether you're reading this as a 20-year-old or a 60-year-old, you have the time and opportunity to change things.

Make informed decisions to improve and strengthen your financial future.

Ladies, we are all worth it.

We deserve it.

Be ambitious.

Dare To Be Fair.

Recommended Reading List

Criado Perez, Caroline. *Invisible Women: Exposing Data Bias in a World Designed by Men*, Vintage/Penguin Random House, 2020

Somerset Webb, Merryn. *Love Is Not Enough: The Smart Woman's Guide to Money*, Harper Press, 2007

Gratton, Lynda & Scott, Andrew. *The 100-Year Life: Living and Working in an Age of Longevity*, Bloomsbury, 2016

Sandberg, Sheryl. *Lean In: Women, Work and the Will to Lead*, WH Allen/Penguin Random House, 2015

Housel, Morgan. *The Psychology of Money: Timeless Lessons on Wealth, Greed and Happiness*, Harriman House, 2020

Endnotes

Introduction

1. Jane Portas, Insuring Women's Futures research, published by the Chartered Insurance Institute, 2019: www.6momentsthatmatter.com

Chapter 1

1. Jane Portas, Living a financially resilient life in the UK, published by the Chartered Insurance Institute, 2019: www.6momentsthatmatter.com

2. ONS 2017 divorce rate, latest data available.

3. Jane Portas, Living a financially resilient life in the UK beyond Covid-19, published by the Chartered Insurance Institute, Nov 2020.

Chapter 2

1. Statista.com

2. Financial Times, April 2019

Chapter 3

1. The Money Advice Service: https://www.moneyadviceservice. org.uk/en/corporate/uk-couples-financial-secrets-revealed

Chapter 6

1. Harvard Business Review, research by Benjamin Artz, Amanda Goodall, Andrew J. Oswald, June 2018.

Chapter 7

1. City Women: https://www.citywomen.co.uk/wp-content/uploads/2014/04/gender-equality-timeline.pdf

2. Parliament: https://www.parliament.uk/about/living-heritage/transformingsociety/electionsvoting/womenvote/overview/thevote/#:~:text=Representation%20of%20the%20People%20Act,a%20property%20qualification%20to%20vote.&text=The%20same%20Act%20abolished%20property,over%20the%20age%20of%2021.

3. Parliament: https://www.parliament.uk/about/living-heritage/transformingsociety/electionsvoting/womenvote/parliamentary-collections/nancy-astor/parliament-qualification-of-women-act/

4. Legislation.gov: https://www.legislation.gov.uk/ukpga/Geo5/9-10/71/section/1

5. Cambridge Family Law Practice: http://www.cflp.co.uk/a-brief-history-of-divorce/

6. Legislation.gov: https://www.legislation.gov.uk/ukpga/Geo5/15-16/20

7. Api.parliament: https://api.parliament.uk/historic-hansard/commons/1956/jun/19/civil-service-equal-pay

8. Women's Legal Landmarks: https://womenslegallandmarks.com/2017/08/08/married-womens-property-act-1964/#:~:text=The%20effect%20of%20the%20Married,so%20reverted%20back%20to%20him.

9. Legislation.gov: https://www.legislation.gov.uk/ukpga/1967/87/contents

10. Parliament https://www.parliament.uk/about/living-heritage/transformingsociety/private-lives/relationships/collections1/

parliament-and-the-1960s/national-health-service-family
-planning-act/

11. Work Smart: https://worksmart.org.uk/jargon-buster/sex-discrimination-act

12. Parliament: https://www.parliament.uk/about/living-heritage/transformingsociety/private-lives/relationships/overview/wedlock-or-deadlock/

13. Margaret Thatcher Foundation: https://www.margaretthatcher.org/document/111449

14. Bailii: http://www.bailii.org/uk/cases/UKHL/1991/12.html

15. Legislation.gov: https://www.legislation.gov.uk/uksi/1999/3312/contents/made

16. LGBT Plus History Month: https://lgbtplushistorymonth.co.uk/wp-content/uploads/2020/02/1384014531S28Background.pdf

17. Legislation.gov: https://www.legislation.gov.uk/ukdsi/2014/9780111118856

18. OECD stands for Organisation for Economic Co-operation and Development. Source - Dominique Anxo – Växjö University: https://www.jil.go.jp/english/reports/documents/jilpt-reports/no.7_anxo.pdf

19 Jane Portas, Insuring Women's Futures research, published by the Chartered Insurance Institute, 2019: www.6momentsthatmatter.com

Resources

To download the resources within the book and find out more about my work, please visit:

www.dare2befair.com

Within this book, I reference research and concepts authored and created by Jane Portas in her Women's Risks in Life Report Series, first published by Insuring Women's Futures, including its Manifesto, 'Living a financially resilient life in the UK - The Moments That Matter in improving women's and all of our financial futures'. This includes actions that may be taken by people, the third sector, employers, guidance bodies, financial services firms, regulators and policymakers to close the women's financial resilience gap.

The Manifesto contains two pledges: the Financial Flexible Working Pledge aimed at employers supporting their employees to consider financial matters on changing work arrangements, and the Inclusive Customer Financial Lives Pledge aimed at financial services firms to prompt their customers to consider their life circumstances when taking out financial products. These pledges are designed to address gaps identified in the research findings.

You can get involved in the workstreams or follow progress on social media.

You can sign up your organisation to the Financial Flexible Working Pledge:

> *"We will work to ensure that at every point where our employees make a change to their working arrangements, they are prompted to consider the immediate and longer-term financial implications of this change."*

And/or the Inclusive Customer Financial Lives Pledge:

> *"We will work to ensure that at every customer interaction point we adopt an inclusive 'whole customer' approach, helping customers to consider the impact of their life circumstances and potential changes, and empowering them to achieve a positive outcome."*

These initiatives are both supported with a Good Practice Guide authored by Jane Portas that can be downloaded from their website:

www.insuringwomensfutures.co.uk

Keep in Touch

I hope reading Dare To Be Fair has opened your eyes to some of the financial disadvantages facing women in their lives. I also hope you're clear on how you can influence and control key aspects of your own financial future, improve workplace practices for more women, and remove or minimise unfairness that still exists.

The checklists and spreadsheets within the book are available to download via my website:

www.dare2befair.com

Above all, this is about starting a bigger conversation amongst women, sharing successes where you have influenced or created change, and inspiring others you know to do the same.

I would love to hear your thoughts, your ideas, and examples of what you've decided to do or change as a result of reading my book.

Please follow me on Instagram @dare2befair and share your stories.

Connect with me on LinkedIn:

www.linkedin.com/in/amanda-redman

My website details other ways of contacting me, including via email:

amanda@dare2befair.com

Thank you for reading and engaging, and good luck!

Printed in Great Britain
by Amazon